Danny Smith's account of Wallenberg's extraordinary exploits, ending in mysterious martyrdom, is a towering, gripping story, told with researched detail and restrained passion. It should be compulsory reading in all our schools, as a reminder of the incomparable evils of Nazism and of the true power of saintly determination. I recommend it to all who wish to learn and to live by a rare example. This latest book, in all its compelling simplicity, provides us with a powerful weapon in the pursuit of the truth about Wallenberg's fate. Wallenberg loved his neighbour as himself. That he should be found alive is the prayer of all of us who find strength in the mirror of his incredible achievements. This book is their definitive and authoritative chronicle.

Lord Janner of Braunstone, QC, The Tablet *(1986)*

Although I have devoted many years of my life to tracking down Nazi war criminals, I consider it even more important to try to find out what happened to Raoul Wallenberg, who is the heroic antithesis of the mass killers ... I don't know anybody better than Raoul Wallenberg to be presented as a model to young people. *Simon Wisenthal, Nazi hunter (1981)*

Wallenberg will never be forgotten in the annals of Israel. He placed his own life in jeopardy, day in and day out, in order to continue his rescue efforts. Raoul Wallenberg, the Jewish people is forever in your debt. We shall hand this memory down to our descendants to the generations yet to come, to be cherished always. *Menachem Begin, Prime Minister of Israel 1977–83 and Nobel Prize Winner 1978 (1981)*

Wallenberg saved 100,000 from Hitler's racial holocaust. If 60 others had acted like him, the Nazi murderers would not have had their 6 million victims.

Shihomo Argov, Israeli Ambassador to Great Britain 1979–82 (1982)

A hero and a noble man of biblical dimensions, both in his immortal deeds and in the suffering that he endured and continues to endure in common with so many of the people whose suffering he relieved.

Lord Jacobovits, former Chief Rabbi (1982)

I consider Raoul Wallenberg to be one of those people of the 20th century to whom all of mankind is greatly indebted and ought to be proud of.
Andrei Sakharov (1981)

We failed to secure the release of one of our most notable countrymen, one of our greatest heroes. On the continuing efforts to obtain certainty, one must presume that Wallenberg is still alive, otherwise it would be pointless to pursue the matter. It is very likely that he is still alive.

Tage Erlander, former Prime Minister of Sweden (1981)

He was one of the true heroes of this century and continues to serve as an example to us all.

Bill Clinton, President of the United States 1992–2000 (1998)

How can we comprehend the moral worth of a man who saved tens and tens of thousands of lives ... wherever he is, his humanity burns like a torch.

Ronald Reagan, President of the United States 1980–88 (1981)

The greatest unsung hero of World War II.

BBC TV Man Alive (1980)

He never tired and was at work day and night. He saved human lives, travelled, bargained, threatened the interruption of diplomatic relations, was in consultation with the Hungarian government – in short achieved something that makes him a sort of legendary figure.

Samu Stern, wartime Hungarian Jewish leader (1980)

He stood there, probably feeling the loneliest man in the world, trying to pretend there was something behind him. They could have shot him there and then in the street and nobody would have known about it.

Tommy Lapid, former Director, Israeli Broadcasting Authority (1980)

Here is a man who had the choice of remaining in a secure neutral Sweden when Nazism was ruling Europe. Instead he left this haven and went to what was then one of the most perilous places in Europe. And for what? To save Jews. He won his battle and I feel that in this age when there is so little to believe in – so very little on which our young people can pin their hopes and ideals – he is a person to show to our world which knows so little about him.

Gideon Hausner, Eichmann's prosecutor,
Chairman of Council at Yad Vashem (1980)

LOST HERO

Raoul Wallenberg's Dramatic Quest to Save the Jews of Hungary

DANNY SMITH

HarperCollins*Publishers*

HarperCollins*Religious*
Part of HarperCollins*Publishers*
77–85 Fulham Palace Road, London w6 8jb
www.christian-publishing.com

First published in Great Britain under the title
Wallenberg: Lost Hero in 1986
by Marshall Morgan and Scott Publications Ltd

This edition 2001

3 5 7 9 10 8 6 4 2

A catalogue record for this book
is available from the British Library

ISBN 0 00 711117 7

Printed and bound in Great Britain by
Omnia Books Ltd, Glasgow

This book is dedicated to Jessica, Rachel and Luke
and their friends. My hope and prayer is that the example
of Raoul Wallenberg will be a torch for the future.

He is a shield for all those who take refuge in him.

Psalm 18:30, Revised Standard Version

No one can show greater proof of love, than by the giving of his
life for his friends.

John 15:13, paraphrase

Contents

Acknowledgements

Joan's steadfast support has been an inspiration. Many friends encouraged me; only a few are mentioned here. Thanks to Sue Richards, Dirk Jan Groot, Wanno Haneveld, Mum and Clement, George Verwer, David Alton, Derek Williams, Jim and Aninha Capaldi, Alexandr Ogorodnikov, Craig and Janet Rickards, Yury Belov, John Whittington, Dr Wai Sin Hu, Roley Horowitz, Father Shay Cullen, Emma Foa and Reg Wright. Thanks also to my friends at Jubilee: Rachel Bader, Ann Buwalda, Emily Murray, Mark Rowland, Wilfred Wong.

Many things have changed since this book first appeared in 1986. Still, this real-life detective story is missing one last clue, one final chapter, before the truth can be laid before us. I am grateful to HarperCollins for giving me another chance to remind people about this extraordinary character.

Grateful acknowledgement is made for permission to reprint extracts from *Righteous Gentile* by John Bierman (Allen Lane, 1981) and *Auschwitz* by Dr Miklos Nyiszli (Panther Books Ltd, 1962).

FOREWORD TO THE
SECOND EDITION, 2001
Wallenberg – a Hero in an Age without Heroes
by Congressman Tom Lantos

US Congressman Tom Lantos is the Chairman of the Congressional Human Rights Caucus. He is the only survivor of the Holocaust to be elected to Congress. Born in Budapest, Hungary, Congressman Lantos was twice sent to Nazi 'work camps' during 1944. He escaped and survived in one of Wallenberg's safe houses. He worked with Wallenberg and was active in the anti-Nazi underground. He arrived in the United States in 1947 and has lived in the San Francisco Bay area since 1950. He married Annette Tillemann, his childhood sweetheart. She was also born in Budapest and survived the Holocaust through Wallenberg's efforts.

Lost Hero by Danny Smith is the incredible but true story of Raoul Wallenberg – a Protestant Swede who risked his life to save tens of thousands of Hungarian Jews from extermination by German and Hungarian Nazis in the chaotic closing days of World War II. It is a true portrait, an accurate image of what Wallenberg did. It cannot, however, convey the enormity of the horror that was endured by those who were persecuted, because words are incapable of expressing the anguish, suffering, terror and degradation perpetrated by one set of human beings upon another.

Almost 15 years ago, my wife Annette began the effort to call attention to the magnitude of what Wallenberg did and to win his release from the Soviet Gulag. She, more than anyone else, was responsible for bringing international attention to Raoul

Wallenberg. When we began this effort, we had two goals. Seeing the publication of this book is a bittersweet experience for us.

First, we wanted everyone on the face of this planet to understand that a single individual with courage and principle can stand up to, and defy, and triumph over a gigantic totalitarian system. That objective has been achieved. This book is the most recent victory in that effort. We are delighted that Wallenberg's story will be still further spread, that his remarkable act of heroism, of saving 100,000 innocent lives, will be known by more people.

We have failed in our second objective. That objective was to free Raoul Wallenberg from the Soviet Gulag. The publication of this book reminds us that his fate is still unknown. When Annette and I began our struggle to save Wallenberg, he was alive, he could have been saved. We do not know whether he is still alive today, but many chances have been missed. Many people – and several governments – could have done a great deal to liberate him. But appeasement and unwillingness to take a stand are responsible for the fact that we may never see him again.

This book is the latest evidence, however, that in the deepest and most profound sense Wallenberg lives – whatever his fate in the Soviet prisons. We honour him; we remember him; his story inspires us to become better human beings and more valiant in our struggle to build a better and safer world.

We are honouring a hero in an age which is so profoundly devoid of heroes, a man who voluntarily assumed a daring and dangerous assignment. Many become heroes when heroism is thrust upon them. But Wallenberg went out of his way, leaving behind the comfort and affluence, the safety and security of Stockholm, to go to Budapest – and I know what Budapest was like in those last hellishly ugly months of World War II. Wallenberg put his life on the line day in and day out for people he did not know because he believed in the right of every human being to live.

Neither I, nor my wife, nor our children, nor our grandchildren would be here today if it were not for Raoul Wallenberg. During that whole dark nightmare, no one else directly confronted Nazi cruelty. No one else had the audacity to follow the death marches, to jump in front of guns levelled at Jews, to pull people off deportation trains. Raoul Wallenberg not only saved 100,000 lives, he saved our faith in humanity. In history, one can find many men who have killed 100,000 people. But how many have saved 100,000? Wallenberg has shown us that one individual motivated by a genuine and personal concern for human rights can face evil and triumph; that one person alone can make a difference; that there are genuine heroes to illuminate our age.

◼◼◼

Introduction to the
First Edition, 1986
by Peter Benenson,
Founder of Amnesty International

Towards the end of the last World War, during six months of incredible heroism and ingenuity, Raoul Wallenberg saved the lives of countless thousands from certain death. This modern 'Scarlet Pimpernel' was a well-born Swede; those he saved were not French aristocrats from the Revolutionary guillotine, but Hungarian Jews from the Nazi gas chambers. The 'Scarlet Pimpernel' was a figure of fiction; Wallenberg was a man of flesh, blood and feeling. What he did is more than history – it is a legend. What has happened to him since is a mystery. This exciting and moving book explains the legend and explores the mystery.

No two peoples are more different in national character than the Swedes and the Hungarians. The former are reputedly cold-blooded and sensible, while the latter are hot-blooded and impulsive. Both countries, Hungary and Sweden, found them-selves almost isolated by the Nazi occupation of surrounding lands in the first stages of the war. The Hungarians retained their nominal independence by throwing in their lot with Hitler and sending troops to join the German army on the Russian front. The Swedes kept their traditional neutrality by agreeing to supply the German munition works with large quantities of iron ore and by permitting German troop trains to cross their country to occupied Norway. In 1940, when Britain stood alone, Hitler's victory seemed almost certain. By the summer of 1944, when the vast Russian armies were steadily rolling back the Germans and the Western Allies pushing forward in France and Italy, the situation had changed. Both Sweden and Hungary tried to recover their full independence, the Swedes using the cloak of neutrality to help the West by humanitarian work inside German-occupied Europe, the Hungarians by toppling the pro-German dictator, Horthy, and setting up a wildly nationalistic and weirdly Christian regime under the emblem of the Arrow Cross.

Thus it came about that Raoul Wallenberg, a minor member of the richest family in Sweden, was sent to Budapest, the Hungarian capital, as First Secretary of the Humanitarian Section of the Swedish Legation. Unofficially President Roosevelt's representative, endowed with unlimited funds by American Jewry, he had a certain leverage with the tottering Horthy regime, but what got into the body and soul of this untried young diplomat, God alone knows. With unbelievable energy and courage he threw himself into the role of protector of all the Jews in Hungary, first from systematic deportation to the German death camps and then from maniacal attacks by the Arrow Cross movement.

The turning point in this story — the second part of the book — comes when the Russians, driving into Hungary well ahead of the Western Allies, objected to Wallenberg's work and arrested him. The German decision to liquidate the 10 million Jews in Europe was made in 1941. It was probably known by Allied intelligence soon afterwards, and was certainly known by reports from the Red Cross, neutral diplomats and escaping Jews early in 1942. The three main Allies, Britain, the USA and Soviet Russia, each reacted with almost unbelievable callousness. The British feared that any attempt to rescue the Jews would bring a mass exodus to their Mandate in Palestine, upsetting both the fragile balance with the Arabs there and Islamic opinion in the British-dominated Middle East. The US government turned away from the prospect of offering large-scale entry visas into what was once the refuge of freedom but now strictly controlled immigration. It was only in 1944 that Franklin Roosevelt, depending on the Jewish vote for re-election to his fourth term as President, started a campaign to save the European Jews. But by then almost all the Jewish communities in Europe had been deported to the east and stood in the wake, not of the American armies, but of the Russian.

Stalin, no great lover of the Jews at the best of times, realized that as his armies moved relentlessly westwards, he would find himself stranded with most of the 4 million Jews who survived the Holocaust. Faced with this prospect, Stalin issued certain orders; what they exactly were we still do not know. At the least, they involved stopping all those who were trying to help the Jews. Raoul Wallenberg was arrested very shortly after the Russians liberated Budapest, apparently on a charge of spying. He was certainly taken to Moscow and to prison there. What has happened to him since remains a most appalling mystery. At the age of 73, he may or may not be still alive. The Kremlin, answering enquiries from Sweden, has issued three self-contradicting stories of his death, yet the evidence of several released prisoners suggests that he was seen in prisons, an Arctic labour camp and a psychiatric hospital during the next 20 years.

The author of this powerful book sets out the Russian statements and the contrary evidence fairly and clearly. It is the latest event in a growing movement of TV documentaries, petitions and organized letter-writing, for, there being no certainty that Wallenberg is dead, Amnesty International has rightly adopted him as a Prisoner of Conscience. The book's publication comes at the time when Gorbachev presents his country with a new image of practicality and change. It is to be hoped that he will give the necessary instructions to reveal the full truth of what has happened to this amazingly brave man in the 40 years since he was arrested. If he does not, the legend of Raoul Wallenberg will continue to grow so that in the end the achievement of the Red Army in liberating Budapest will pale into the mist of history; what will be remembered will be the haunting figure of one young, blond, inspired Swede who deserves the title of the 'bravest of the brave'.

Part One

MISSION

Chapter 1

❖❖❖

A Swedish Diplomat
on a Secret Mission

On the road to Auschwitz, 1944

He steps from the shadows like some subterranean saviour, appearing at the midnight hour, when all hope has gone and fear freezes every heart. Clutching a book of life, he moves swiftly through the mass of people huddled together in a dark, foreboding brick outhouse at the Austrian border.

Dressed in a black leather coat and a fashionable fur-lined hat, he appears unimpressively inconsequential, at times almost insignificant. But it is a deceptive disguise. He addresses the group of women, speaking in a soft voice. 'I want to help you all, but please forgive me: I can only save a few. I feel I have a mission to save the Jewish nation.' He continues the soliloquy, still delivered in hushed tones. 'I must save the young. I have so little time...'

Glancing around the darkened room, he absorbs the pitiful scene. Hungarian Jewesses, young girls and older women, have collapsed with exhaustion after a tormenting 120-mile march from the capital city of Budapest. Weak from dysentery, parched and hungry, marked by the dust and dirt of the journey, over-run by lice, with no privacy for personal sanitation, they have stumbled into this last outpost at the Austrian border. Soon, they will be herded like cattle marked for the slaughterhouse, aboard freight trains headed for the concentration camps. A yellow star is pinned to their breast, the emblem of their death.

He can tell that many of these women have been wealthy, proud, untouched by the circumstances of neighbouring Jews in Europe. They seem in a daze, their eyes aghast, shocked. They stare uncomprehendingly ahead, mute, overwhelmed by the threat of impending doom. Not believing what they have seen and experienced, trapped in some psychotic nightmare, they appear strangely without shame, almost beyond hope.

At once they recognize him. His legend precedes him. 'It's Wallenberg,' one elderly woman whispers. 'Save us, please save us. We're going to die.' The cry ricochets around the barn, as united their voices raise a pitiful plea, imploring this man of mystery to wave a magic wand and return them to their tranquil lives.

The death march from Budapest has shattered their last vestige of dignity. As if in a trance, they surge forward, helpless to resist the taunts and curses of Gestapo guards and Hungarian gendarmes. Tired stragglers are smashed in the back with rifle butts. Those unable to keep pace collapse, falling in the slush and mud of the roadside, abandoned to an unmarked grave. Newspapers cover some bodies.

In freezing rain, the pathetic column forges a stark trail across the Hungarian landscape, passing stone houses beside country lanes. Flashes of forked lightning accompany a thunderous crescendo, crackling across the heavens, as if wailing for those who are unable to weep and tolling for those who have fallen.

Although the Jews of Europe had been systematically wiped out by Hitler's dreaded Gestapo, and rumours of the Third Reich's 'Final Solution' were circulating, the Jewish community in Hungary firmly believed this terror would never reach them. It was all to change with the midnight knock on the door. Mothers clutched babies to their breast as they climbed on to tarpaulin-covered trucks. Those who resisted got a bullet in the back of the head. And, finally, there were the death marches to the Austrian border. Their worst fears were confirmed; there would be no escape from the executioner's net.

Even Raoul Wallenberg is unprepared for the scene inside the barn. He appears visibly shocked and flinches from time to time at the degradation and humiliation of fellow human beings. The images will never leave his mind – women like animals awaiting slaughter.

He forces himself around the barn with one arm still clutching the black book, opening it frequently to jot down the names of those to whom he speaks. He repeats his words for those in the far corner of the barn to hear. 'Please forgive me. You must forgive me. I wish I could help you all. I have a mission to save the Jewish nation. I can only save a few hundred, and I must save the young.'

Amidst the stench and sweat and cluster of bodies, each straining to catch his eye, he sees a young woman in a dark corner of the barn. She lies on the cold, damp ground where she has crawled. She feels faint, unable to move, as if all strength has left her body. Although she is young, barely 17, the march from Budapest, and the appalling sights she witnessed, have virtually suffocated the life and soul out of her.

Despite a tremendous will to survive, she is unable to summon her senses and command her body to rise and appeal to this mysterious figure. She watches him closely and follows his every movement until their eyes meet for a sparkling instant. 'I didn't think he could do anything,' she recalls. 'I remember being struck by how handsome he looked and how clean – in his leather coat and fur hat, just like a being from another world, and I thought, why does he bother with such wretched creatures as we?'

When she heard him speak of 'saving the Jewish nation' her heart fluttered. 'I had never heard the idea of a Jewish nation before. Jewish people, of course, but not a Jewish nation.' At the time Hitler's Final Solution threatened, the Third Reich's target was the total annihilation of 11 million European Jews.

He carefully steps across the bodies lying in the barn and delicately positions himself over her fallen frame. Like some movie hero, he stoops down to stare directly into her face. His eyes are kind, gentle. 'What is your name?' His voice is soothing, comforting. She feels he can see beyond her shame and humilia-tion. She whispers in reply, trying to make herself heard above the clamour aroused by his presence in the barn. He balances the book in one hand and quickly scrawls across its page with his silver pen.

Miriam Herzog...

In a flash he is gone, but the memory of the moment exerts a hypnotic power that has never left her mind. The encounter lasted a few seconds. It was to save Miriam Herzog's life and she would be unable to forget those precious few seconds.

Another young woman, Susan Tabor, was also cast beneath the shadow of the legendary Wallenberg, on another occasion. 'He made me feel human again. For the first time I had hope. In fact, I think that everyone felt different after his first visit. He showed us that we were not animals, that someone cared about us. And the point of it was that he came himself, he came personally. He stopped for us, for each of us...'

The legend of Raoul Wallenberg reached epic proportions during the brutal death marches, engineered by the notorious Adolf Eichmann, during which thousands of Hungarian Jews perished.

Many like Miriam Herzog were literally snatched from the jaws of death by personal encounters with the Swedish diplomat. Everyone within reach received safe passage, by means of pass-ports, travel cards, fictitious documents, a driving licence, some-times merely scraps of paper.

He pursued the hunted and the doomed with the passion of a man 'commissioned by God'. There were no limits to his reckless-ness. Empowered with a charismatic presence, he engaged in combat with the evil forces of Nazism and refused to surrender his licence to save Jews.

Raoul Wallenberg was sent to Hungary in 1944 on a secret assignment handed down by the American President Franklin Roosevelt in the final days of Hitler's genocide. Wallenberg's mission — simply, to rescue Jews! Somewhere in the streets of

Budapest in 1944, this became a personal campaign, with Wallenberg a solitary figure in combat with his adversary Adolf Eichmann. Both men, charged with a burning sense of history, posed a classic challenge of good and evil in a world ablaze.

Budapest is bombarded daily with heavy shelling by the invading Red Army. Buildings are hit and crumble. Bodies lie in the street where they have been slain. A wave of lawlessness is unleashed. Armed gangs roam the streets of Budapest terrorizing the innocent. Even though the war is virtually over, the Jews are tracked down and murdered. In one grisly game, three Jews are handcuffed together and lined up beside the Danube, flowing serenely along. The middle Jew is shot in the back and plunges headlong into the icy water, dragging both screaming men along with him. Sadistic laughter follows, as the two heads bob up and down, struggling to stay afloat, while the attached corpse drags them down. On occasions, a young fascist terrorist takes pot shots at the writhing heads, until they finally disappear beneath the surface of the Danube.

The price on Wallenberg's head has increased as gunmen and bounty hunters are reminded of the contract on his life. Hunted by the Gestapo and by the fascist government's thugs, he goes underground. On the run, he changes apartments each night, alert to the danger whenever he steps into the street.

Wallenberg, warned that he is the most wanted man in Pest, is urged to take shelter with the other neutral diplomats in the relatively calmer environment of Buda, Pest's twin city across the Danube. He shakes his head. 'No, my friend,' he says. 'I cannot leave my Jews.' Through the underground, Wallenberg has learned that Eichmann plans a final massacre of the entire Jewish population in Hungary, now corralled together into a central 'international ghetto'. 'If I leave,' Wallenberg argues, 'there will be nothing to stop Eichmann from fulfilling this final act of madness. I must stay.'

Wallenberg senses that, with the Russian army closing on Budapest, he can complete his mission and save the Jews. If he can somehow hang on. It is a desperate race against time. Every day counts.

Finally, liberation comes in the first few days of January 1945, and the echo of Russian troops can be heard as they trample the cobblestone streets around the town square. Eichmann and the Gestapo have fled overnight, each plotting their own escape, some through the Odessa network.

Unknown to Raoul Wallenberg, however, he has crossed an unmarked, invisible line, where he is cast as an unsuspecting actor in a deadly game, orchestrated by an unseen hand. Plucked from this theatre of war, he is to disappear into the midnight terror of Russia's prison world, trapped alive in a real-life Kafkaesque drama, with no exit and no one to hear his cry.

For six months he has played a cat-and-mouse game with Eichmann and the Third Reich, staying one step ahead, protected by some hidden force, some guardian angel. But now time is running out for Raoul Wallenberg.

For Wallenberg, 17 January 1945 was a new morning. The sun striking through an overcast sky left a sliver of ice on treacherously slippery pavements. Inside the Swedish-protected house at 6 Tatra Street, he talked to his trusted colleagues, many of whom had shared perilous experiences with him during the past six months of German occupation under Eichmann.

The leader of the house, Rezso Muller, strides into the first-floor room as soon as he hears that Wallenberg has arrived. Eagerly they exchange news about individuals and families who have escaped and are still in hiding in secret coves around the city. They are joined shortly by Laszlo Peto, a boyhood friend of the Swedish diplomat.

Raoul Wallenberg is aglow with anticipation. He has won a momentous victory. The Jews of Budapest — about 100,000 — have been saved, largely through his intervention and influence. They constitute the only surviving Jewish remnant alive in Europe after the war. He explains that he is on his way to Debrecen, about 120 miles to the east, where Marshall Malinovsky's conquering Red Army have set up their headquarters.

The Swedish diplomat is concerned about feeding 'his Jews' and keeping the soup kitchens, safe houses and hospitals under his care well supplied with food. He is also keen to share his plans for the economic recovery and restoration of Hungary. He explains that he has already established contact with the Russians and has been given a three-man escort who will personally accompany him to Debrecen. He speaks animatedly and with an air of excitement. Perhaps he senses that history and God have spared him to savour this moment of destiny.

Wallenberg walks to the first-floor window and glances across Tatra Street. There is still a chill in the air and he winces slightly as he peers through the open window. Amidst the rubble and dust of the street, his faithful Hungarian driver, Vilmos Langfelder, can be seen checking the oil on the diplomat's Studebaker, readying the flashy American car for the 120-mile journey. The Red Army's motorcycle escort is parked in front of the Studebaker, also waiting for their charge.

Muller and other members of his staff are alarmed about Wallenberg's intended journey. The streets are unsafe. Snipers on rooftops and in alleys are picking out last-minute victims. If he is spotted by any fascist gunmen, he will be an immediate target.

'There's still a contract on your life. Why take chances?' Muller argues. 'Besides, the Russians are shelling the city. We can feel the tremors right inside this house.'

The others in the room agree, sensing danger. Everyone in the room owes him a personal debt and have survived only because of Wallenberg's personal intervention. 'Wait in Budapest. The Russian army will be here in a few days. It's too risky,' Muller implores him.

But Wallenberg is impatient. He dismisses their well-intentioned caution. Anyway, he has the protection of Major Dimitri Demchinkov and there is urgent business to finalize, which he outlines once again. He must obtain food for 'his Jews' and the Russians must be told to stop shelling the area where the Swedish Legation is situated, as innocent lives are at risk.

'I'll be safe,' he insists. 'After all, I've survived the last six months. What can possibly happen to me now?' He pauses for a moment. 'I'll be back in about 10 days, by the end of January or early February. You can be sure of that.'

Wallenberg opens his briefcase and takes out a bundle of banknotes. He counts out 100,000 pengös and hands it over to Rezso Muller, 'for food and expenses'.

It was well known that Wallenberg carried large sums of money around with him and also had money hidden in his car. At the time, he was also conveying additional jewellery and valuables to Debrecen. He never explained why.

Wallenberg stretched, stifling a yawn. His staff knew how much he had pushed himself during these last few weeks and just how tired he was. Through the window he could now see the Russian soldiers standing by their motorcycles. Pausing for a moment, he jerked his head in their direction. 'Can you see my escort? I don't know if they are watching me or protecting me. I'm not sure if I'm their guest or their prisoner.' It was a prophetic joke that was to have a chilling aftermath.

After some last-minute consultations, he waved goodbye to Muller and his other colleagues and stepped into Tatra Street and gestured to the Russian soldiers. Wallenberg climbed into the Studebaker with Vilmos Langfelder at the wheel, accompanied by Laszlo Peto, who had decided to go with Raoul on the long journey ahead. But as their convoy was leaving the centre of town, he changed his mind and decided to remain in Budapest.

Laszlo climbed out of the Studebaker on the corner of Benczur Street. He stood on the cracked, icy pavement and, with the car door wide open, the two men clasped hands firmly. Wallenberg was in 'a great mood, a brilliant mood'. Vilmos moved the car into first gear, followed by Major Demchinkov and the armed Russian escort on motorbikes.

Lazslo turned and walked in the direction of one of the Swedish safe houses. All his thoughts were with his parents across the Danube in Pest. They were hiding underground and Laszlo had heard the Russians say they would be liberating Pest very soon. Anxiously, his thoughts were concentrated on their safety and he had decided he would remain behind and try to trace them.

On impulse, Laszlo glanced round as the Studebaker and its armed escort were pulling away. He raised his arm, waved and turned to walk hurriedly away down a side street.

As he moved, Laszlo caught a fleeting glimpse of Wallenberg, his smiling face at the car window. This image, frozen in time, was to become the final memory of his last hour.

No one would ever see Raoul Wallenberg as a free man again.

Chapter 2

∵∴∵

Discontented Dreamer

Paris, 1942

Raoul Wallenberg had always been something of a dreamer. Yet, in Paris of '42, this roving Swedish aristocrat experienced the first stirrings of a restless discontent.

As a young man, not yet 30 years of age, he whistled the popular tunes of the day, and shyly turned to catch the eye of a shapely young Parisian belle.

Raoul lived on the brink of palatial splendour back home in Sweden. The Wallenberg dynasty embraced diplomats and ambassadors, bankers and bishops, artists and professors, and the family were affectionately referred to as the 'Rockefellers of Sweden'. The Wallenbergs enjoyed the favours of the Royal Palace, partied with high society, and undertook confidential political negotiations representing their country. Although the Wallenberg empire spanned the higher echelons of power and wealth, however, Raoul was somehow excluded from its inner courts.

His father, Raoul Wallenberg Sr, an officer in the Swedish Navy and the son of the Swedish Ambassador to Japan, succumbed to a cancerous tumour three months before the birth of his only child, Raoul Gustav, born on 4 August 1912. At first his mother, a dazzlingly beautiful girl called Maj Wissing, seemed overcome with despair. 'I feel an enormous emptiness inside. I don't know if I will be competent to raise this child,' she confided to her mother.

However, shortly afterwards, her young son caused a remarkable transformation in her attitude. 'I have never known such happiness could exist. He is already taking care of me,' she wrote cheerfully.

His early childhood and teenage years were moulded by his grandfather, Ambassador Gustav Wallenberg. The young man travelled the world, proved himself an exemplary and outstanding student of architecture at the University of Michigan in the USA, and undertook roving assignments in high finance, first in South Africa, and then in 1936 his grandfather arranged an appointment at the Holland Bank in Haifa, Palestine.

Living in a cheap, strictly kosher *pension* on 18 Arlosorof Street, young Raoul swapped stories and philosophies with other residents.

Under British control, the 50,000 or so Jews were unhappy about the protection afforded by the authorities. Anti-Semitism seemed prevalent, even encouraged. Jewish refugees had fled Germany with disturbing stories and sinister rumours. Nazi activists had organized a public burning of Jewish publications and books written by opponents of Nazism, and their leader, Adolf Hitler, was being hailed as a heroic figure.

Ariel Kahane fled Berlin and returned to Palestine to rebuild his life, trying to find employment as an architect. He soon found a sympathetic friend in this young Swedish banker. Years later, Kahane told Elenore Lester, 'We talked late into the night. I was probably the poorest architect of the time, and he was possibly the richest, but we talked on completely equal terms.'

Raoul listened spellbound over candlelit dinners at the boarding house's restaurant, and for the first time he heard first-hand from young Jewish men and women, their faces tense and frightened, about the discrimination and abuse they experienced.

He remained a dutiful and attentive apprentice, but was he destined to spend the rest of his days locked in a vault at the centre of some real-life Monopoly game? The thought was repugnant. In some anxiety, he wrote to his grandfather and guardian, Ambassador Wallenberg:

To tell the truth I don't feel especially bankish; a bank president should have something judge-like and calm about him and moreover be cool and cynical. Freund [his boss in Haifa] and Jacob W [his cousin] are no doubt typical and I myself feel as different from them as I possibly could. I think it is more in my nature to work positively for something than to sit around telling people, 'no!'

His cousin Jacob Wallenberg controlled the family's Enskilda Bank and remained at the helm of the Wallenberg empire. Jacob's brother Marcus also played a significant role in the distribution of power.

Although they gave him short-term assignments, the Wallenbergs could find no desk space for their wandering cousin Raoul, as he remained outside the family's influence. Jacob and Marcus were established at the helm of the business and destined to play an important role during the coming turbulent years of war. Having a famous name such as Wallenberg counted for little to Raoul as a young man. Little did anyone realize what a devastating effect this name was to have in deciding his fate.

With negligible help from the clan, Raoul embarked on a new career as an entrepreneur. He teamed up with a Hungarian Jew, Koloman Lauer, who ran an import-export business trading in food between Sweden and Central Europe. With the sinister net of Nazism spreading, Lauer identified a useful purpose for his new 'trade representative', and in January 1942 the young Wallenberg found himself yet again on assignment, this time in Paris.

The glamour and the bright lights of Paris nightlife were marred as his business contacts thrust him into day-to-day contact with the Jewish community, inevitably at the centre of business life.

France itself was under German occupation and Adolf Eichmann was busy establishing his reputation as an efficient, though ruthless, exponent of Nazi policy.

Concentration camps had been constructed at Dachau, Buchenwald and Auschwitz – their names destined to become symbols of evil. Some deportations had started from France and a street-by-street survey had already decided the fate of 3,619 native Polish Jews, who had been moved to primitive internment camps controlled by sadistic French guards. An increasing death rate from starvation, cold, disease and abuse in the camps was alarming the Jews of France.

Two Paris synagogues were targets for attempted bombings and the Jewish community was faced with a fine of a billion francs. In a few days, French Jews were to be subject to another humiliation and forced to wear a yellow star displayed on the outer jacket of their clothes.

Raoul Wallenberg's assignment in Paris brought him into direct contact with the problems facing French Jews, and the brooding images revived the stories he had first heard over those candlelit dinners in a Haifa *pension*. The Jews of Europe, he thought, what is to become of them?

Berlin, 1942

Unknown to him, an influential council of power was posing the same question in an elegant Berlin suburb. One man in their midst had already given them the answer. *Extermination!*

The Final Solution had already been approved. The practical details were being worked out.

On 20 January 1942, a conference held in a spacious villa on the outskirts of Berlin was to determine the future of the Jews of Europe. The Wannsee Conference was aimed at co-ordinating agencies within the government and it was attended by 16 high-level officials from the State and Party representing Foreign Affairs, Justice, the Interior, the Four-Year Plan and the Reich Chancellery.

SS General Reinhard Heydrich, nicknamed 'the blond beast', eased back his leather chair and stood up facing the 16 officers who had assembled in the stately room. By his side, the head of the

Gestapo's Section IV B4 for Jewish Affairs, Lieutenant-Colonel Adolf Eichmann, sat attentively with a pad and pen neatly placed in front of him. His moment had come. Eichmann had worked his way through the ranks and risen to considerable power within the SS. His special talents in efficient administration, organization and logistics were proven effective. He had worked hard for this meeting and had prepared the agenda for the conference. Sixteen copies, together with briefing and background papers, had been neatly laid out for the representatives of State, police and SS.

Heydrich was not a charismatic speaker like Adolf Hitler, but his words carried the influence and, most importantly, the authority of the *Führer*. He was Hitler's spokesman. Everyone had better pay attention!

'Gentlemen, thank you for coming. You know why we are here.' Skipping easily through the preliminaries, Heydrich introduced each of the 16 representatives. Eichmann smiled and bowed slightly, as his role in this conference was acknowledged.

Some senior SS men knew what Heydrich was about to say. A few days earlier, he had summoned the Commandant of Auschwitz, Rudolf Hoess, and confided that Hitler had bestowed on him an awesome commission.

Now he stood before the assembled officers and in a calm and relaxed voice said, 'Our beloved *Führer* has given me a solemn responsibility. I have been charged with bringing about a complete solution of the Jewish question in the German sphere of influence in Europe.'

No one stirred as Heydrich continued, 'Europe is to be combed from the east to the west. We must clear up the situation, group by group. We are going to solve the Jewish problem once and for all.' He paused and then, with a flourish, added, 'Finally, Europe will be *Judenrein* [Jew-free]!'

The 16 German officers listened in attentive silence. The room felt suddenly claustrophobic. Eichmann sat on the edge of his chair, listening intently to every word.

Heydrich went on with his prolonged but effective speech, pausing for his words to sink in fully, faltering for a moment while searching for a word to describe the ultimate fate of the Jewish population. 'It's an ambitious project. Millions of people will have to be traced, catalogued, apprehended, assembled, and then...' again he paused in mid-sentence. 'Then ... deported,' he continued more confidently, 'and resettled,' he said with finality.

Heydrich continued to speak about the *Führer's* command, explaining that the task had fallen to the SS to fulfil this order and complete the 'resettlement programme', clearly a euphemism for extermination. He turned to Eichmann, sitting impassively by his side, and said, 'We are grateful to Herr Eichmann for his efforts in preparing the agenda for our conference and all these valuable papers.' Heydrich was referring to a series of documents listing the numbers of Jews in each European country.

'Our target for the resettlement programme is 11 million people.' He spoke the words with confidence and authority, echoing the emphasis that the *Führer* himself had imposed on the task ahead. 'It's going to be quite an operation, my friends, but we have the capabilities and the genius to accomplish this assignment. It will be a momentous occasion, and our role in such a historic venture will not be forgotten in the years to come.'

After his speech, the delegates engaged in animated discussion. Questions about the fate of part-Jews had to be decided. Heydrich remained silent as some extremists argued that the policy should cover everyone. Few realized that Heydrich himself had a Jewish grandmother in his ancestry.

The strategy of the Final Solution had been in operation for over a year, and already well over a million people had fallen victim to machine-gun squads that swept Russia, and to vicious pogroms throughout Poland.

If anyone at the Wannsee Conference felt daunted by the sheer physical task of annihilating 11 million people, their fears were quickly allayed. Although some Gestapo officers at the conference had been informed, the entire group were virtually silent to a man as the outline of an inventive strategy was presented to them.

Jews were to be located and catalogued before the deportations began. The healthy ones would be used as slave labour for the war effort. It was the least they could do, the conference was reminded. After all, there was a war on.

But the mammoth task of disposing of the bodies? Just how could that be accomplished effectively?

It was at this point that the conference moved into a second gear, with inventive contributions from Eichmann, who had prepared himself for this moment and now began to dominate the proceedings. He spoke as someone who clearly relished his assignment. Heydrich had been given command of the extermination, but Eichmann was the master architect.

The technology of genocide was being hitched to the machinery already assembled. The wagons were being harnessed and readied and marched to the starting posts. Some final tinkering and fine-tuning was all that was required.

On 1 March 1941, Himmler had arrived in Auschwitz and, following a survey of the land, had ordered the construction of a concentration camp. It was to become 'the largest slaughterhouse history has ever known', according to the Camp Commandant, Rudolf Hoess. He explained, 'The existing extermination points in the east were inadequate for large-scale, long-term activity and I designated Auschwitz for this purpose.'

Despite complaints that drainage difficulties and problems caused by lack of water would hinder the plan, Himmler was adamant. At a senior staff meeting he declared, 'Gentlemen, it will be built. My reasons for construction are far more important than your objections.'

In the autumn of 1941, Russian prisoners of war arrived in Auschwitz following secret orders for their arrest issued by Hitler. They were lined up side by side in the gravel pit near the monopoly buildings, where articles of clothes and equipment for the SS rank and file were stored. One by one, the Russian soldiers were executed.

One night, Fritzsch, Hoess's deputy at Auschwitz, ordered a group of Russian soldiers into one of the underground detention cells in the camp's buildings. Did they glance at one another with a glimmer of hope?

Fritzsch then donned a gas mask and, clutching a canister of gas, discharged it into the cell.

Taken by surprise, the soldiers clutched their throats and clawed at the air, like actors in some bizarre pantomime. Those by the walls and door of the cell slammed their fists and bodies at the concrete and wood. In a few seconds, the dull, lifeless bodies collapsed in heaps on the floor of the cell. When it was over, this success was reported directly to Hoess.

The camp at Auschwitz had stumbled onto something unusual, perhaps even historic. Inspired by its potential, Hoess insisted that another experiment be set up. He wanted to see things personally.

The very next transportation of Russian POWs were marched directly to the detention cells of Building II. Hoess recalls, 'Protected by a gas mask, I watched the killing myself. A short, almost smothered cry, and it was all over. During this first experience of gassing people I did not fully realize what was happening, perhaps because I was too impressed by the whole procedure.'

Preoccupied by the techniques, Hoess found the death of these Russians soldiers difficult to recall when writing his memoirs. Soon after this, Auschwitz's old crematorium opened its doors and 900 Russian prisoners, yet another shipment, were marched straight into the concrete mortuary 'to be deloused'. Of this event, Hoess writes, 'I have a clearer recollection. When the powder was thrown in, there were cries of "gas", then a great bellowing, and then trapped prisoners hurled themselves against both the doors. But the doors held.'

Confident that the venture was successful, Hoess notes matter-of-factly, 'The killing of these Russian prisoners of war did not cause me much concern at the time. The order had been given, and I had to carry it out.'

The gas, in fact, was Cyclon B, an amethyst-blue crystal, its name taken from the abbreviation of its essential elements: cyanide, chlorine and nitrogen. Cyclon B was manufactured by the firm of I.G. Farben Co. during the war as a disinfectant for the destruction of rats, cockroaches and other vermin that infected the camp. The boxes of Cyclon B were labelled 'Poison: for the destruction of parasites'. It was manufactured in large quantities and could be stored in dry, solid canisters or drums. The stock of Cyclon B in Auschwitz was never held in the crematorium itself, but before the gassings a car, provided by the International Red Cross, would carry canisters of the deathly gas to the crematorium. The pellets acted instantly, as they turned to gas when exposed to the air.

Dr Miklos Nyiszli, a Hungarian doctor forced to assist Josef Mengele, noted, 'For every convoy it was the same. Red Cross cars brought the gas from the outside. There was never a stock of it in the crematorium. The precaution was scandalous, but still more scandalous was the fact that the gas was brought in a car bearing the insignia of the International Red Cross.' During the Nuremberg trials, the Farben Company claimed that Cyclon B had been manufactured only as a disinfectant. However, Dr Nyiszli pointed out in his testimony that there were two types of Cyclon gas in production. They came in identical containers; only the markings 'A' and 'B' identified them. Type 'A' was a disinfectant; type 'B' was used to exterminate millions.

News of the experiments carried out by Hoess and Fritzsch in Auschwitz with Cyclon B spread with increasing excitement throughout the SS. It was the breakthrough they needed. Hoess was summoned to Berlin in the summer of 1941, just months before the Wannsee Conference. In a private office alone with Himmler, he was told, 'The *Führer* has ordered that the Jewish question be solved once and for all and that we, the SS, are to implement that order. The Jews are the sworn enemies of the German people and must be eradicated. Every Jew that we can lay our hands on is to be destroyed.' Eichmann was so excited about the experiments that he visited Auschwitz personally to hear first-hand about the effects of Cyclon B. Hoess recalls in his memoirs, 'We decided to employ it for the mass extermination operation. Now we had the gas, and we had established a procedure.'

The Wannsee Conference was deemed an overwhelming success. The 16 assembled Reich leaders were now confident that the almost impossible target of the elimination of 11 million European Jews could be achieved. As Hoess had indicated, they had the gas and Auschwitz had proclaimed its effectiveness.

'And so, gentlemen. This is the end of the conference,' Heydrich concluded. 'The end of a historic meeting – yes, a milestone in our history. When Europe has been conquered and is finally Jew-free, we will all remember this historic day, 22 January 1942. Now, it's time to toast our *Führer*.'

An orderly was dispatched to organize the drinks and a festive spirit permeated the group. Despite the shortages caused by the war, a grand spread of food and liqueurs was procured for those attending the Wannsee Conference. Heydrich, Gestapo chief Müller and Eichmann lingered by the warm fireside, discussing past triumphs and future conquests.

When Eichmann recalled the event in an interview with a Dutch journalist in Argentina, his nostalgic recollections were of a group singing and drinking. 'After a while we got up on the chairs and drank a toast, then on the table and then round and round – on the chairs and on the table again. Heydrich taught it to us. It was an old North German custom. But we sat around peacefully after our Wannsee Conference, not just talking shop, but giving ourselves a rest after so many taxing hours.'

Eichmann could barely conceal his excitement at the outcome of the Wannsee Conference. Warmed by the challenge, he saw the potential for establishing his reputation as 'a fantastic opportunity'.

Heydrich may have been given the responsibility by the *Führer*, but Eichmann was at the controls. There was not a moment to lose. Time was running out for the Jews of Europe.

Chapter 3

❖❖❖

No One Escapes from Auschwitz Alive

Stockholm, 1942

Dressed in a smart, steel-grey business suit, the young entrepreneur Raoul Wallenberg enjoyed the politics of negotiation as he travelled in Nazi-occupied France, Germany and Hungary during the early forties. During his travels he observed the increasing hostility towards Jews.

A man about town, he dated several attractive young women. He disliked team sports, exercised regularly and kept physically fit, while enjoying the inheritance of his grandfather's wine collection. His bachelor lifestyle was etched in comfort and ease and his only direct encounter with the world at war occurred when he ventured out on business trips around Europe. In neutral Sweden he was removed from danger, remote from the tragedy of human experience now touching millions of lives. Someone who knew him at the time recalls that on occasions he appeared depressed, noting, 'I had the feeling he wanted to do something more worthwhile with his life.'

One winter evening in 1942, Raoul and his half-sister Nina attended a private showing of the film *Pimpernel Smith* at the British Embassy in Stockholm. The film portrayed the story of an absent-minded professor, played by the noted British actor Leslie Howard (by some twist of fate a Hungarian Jew in real life), who manages to save Jews from the Nazis. The film was based on Baroness

Orczy's novel *The Scarlet Pimpernel.* On the way home that evening, Raoul and Nina began discussing the film. Speaking almost prophetically, Raoul told her, 'That's just the kind of thing I'd like to do.'

His own personal future seemed precarious. There was still no indication that the gates to the Wallenberg empire were about to open to him. Lacking the support of a father to care for his welfare, he had already suffered the loss of a benevolent grandfather.

Ventures into the business world proved less than spectacular. He was an architect who had, as yet, designed nothing; an entrepreneur without a business; a banker with connections but one who could not do a deal for himself. Even the family industry could not find space for one more Wallenberg. He had not inherited any treasure and was unable to discover any for himself. He was stirred deeply by the tragic experiences of Jews he had heard about and those he encountered but was unable to respond.

Issues of faith were considered a personal matter, but Raoul attended the Lutheran Church and had sung the *Messiah* in the church choir. As a youth, he had come under the influence of an English clergyman, had memorized passages from Scripture, and now, as a young man, he was reminded of the Bible stories about the children of God.

In 1942, at the age of 30, Raoul Wallenberg gave the impression of being a lonesome soul in search of a vision, a man in need of a mission.

Auschwitz

The Wannsee Conference held in January 1942 was to become a landmark in the strategy of the Final Solution.

With the invention of the crystal gas, Cyclon B, human lives were reduced to the level of the vermin for which the gas was originally intended. The very name of Eichmann was becoming a symbol of fear as he continued, with unabated zeal, to work towards the grim target. His victims queued obediently to board the trains that would take them to their deaths. Men, women and children were pulled from their homes and from each other in city after city. They came from Belgium, Bulgaria, Czechoslovakia, France, Germany, Austria, Greece, Holland, Italy, Poland, Romania, Scandinavia and Yugoslavia.

At times, Eichmann seemed propelled by some force of evil. One Protestant clergyman who had gone to him to plead for the life of an individual Jew remarked, 'He was like a piece of ice or marble. Nothing ever touched his heart.'

Rudolf Hoess, the Commandant of Auschwitz, recalled Eichmann as 'a vivacious, active man in his thirties, and always full of energy. He was constantly hatching new plans and perpetually on the lookout for innovations and improvements. He could never rest. He was obsessed with the Jewish question and the order which had been given for its Final Solution.' Eichmann had boasted to a friend, 'I will jump into my grave laughing because the fact that I have the deaths of 5 million Jews on my conscience gives me extraordinary satisfaction.'

In March 1933 the first concentration camp in Nazi Germany had been opened in Dachau. As the operation grew, more camps were opened to accommodate the victims of the purge.

On the platform at Auschwitz, Josef Mengele, who had earned the name 'Angel of Death', conducted his own particular selection process. Sometimes just a nod or a flicker of the eyes were enough to decide someone's fate. Those who survived often ended up as human guinea pigs in the doctor's special laboratory, where he performed a variety of ghoulish experiments in genetics.

In the hope of turning brown eyes to blue, for example, Mengele injected the eyes of children with dyes and poisons. He castrated men, forced miscarriages in women and exposed healthy patients to X-ray radiation and yellow fever. When his experiments were concluded, the majority of his subjects were exterminated. After taking correct medical precautions during childbirth, for example, rigorously observing all aseptic principles, cutting the umbilical cord with consummate care, he would then send the mother and infant to be burned in the crematorium.

Mengele's fascination with twins and dwarfs caused some grisly encounters. At a tribunal in Jerusalem in February 1984, Auschwitz survivors told of twin toddlers who had been stitched together and of how, discovering a Romanian circus family of seven dwarfs, he had exhibited them naked before an audience of 2,000 cheering SS men.

The walls of one of the doctor's laboratories had row upon row of eyes on it 'pinned up like butterflies', one survivor remembered. His sadism could cause even his colleagues to shudder. One observed that 'in Mengele's presence, the SS themselves trembled'.

Mengele greeted each of the new arrivals at Auschwitz in polished boots. Whistling Wagner, he would mark those for the labour camp. The less fortunate travellers were taken directly to the bunkers, forced to undress and then ushered into the chamber of death.

The signs outside the underground gas chambers of the crematorium announced in seven languages, 'Baths'. Another sign at the entrance to the camp read, 'Freedom through work'.

Following the gassing, the women's hair was cut and gold teeth removed. On one occasion, Eichmann told Hoess that the jewellery and currency obtained from their Jewish victims were sold in Switzerland and that the entire Swiss jewellery market was dominated by these sales.

All those who volunteered to help with the operation in the gas chambers, possibly hoping that this might save their lives, were systematically killed, after weeks of a horrible existence. There was to be no respite.

The gassings themselves were appalling. One eyewitness recalls:

The ventilators, patented 'Exhator' system, quickly evacuated the gas from the room, but in the crannies between the dead and the cracks of the doors small pockets of it always remained. Even two hours later it caused a suffocating cough. For that reason the *Sonderkommando* group which first moved into the room was equipped with gas masks. The room was powerfully lighted, revealing a horrible spectacle.

The bodies were not lying here and there throughout the room, but piled in a mass to the ceiling. The reason for this was that the gas first inundated the lower layers of air and rose but slowly towards the ceiling. This forced the victims to trample one another in a frantic effort to escape the gas. Yet a few feet higher up the gas reached them. What a struggle for life there must have been! Nevertheless, it was merely a matter of two or three minutes' respite. If they had been able to think about what they were doing, they would have realized they were trampling their own children, their wives, their relatives. But they couldn't think. Their gestures were no more than the reflexes of the instinct of self-preservation. I noticed that the bodies of the women, the children, and the aged were at the bottom of the pile; at the top, the strongest. Their bodies, which were covered with scratches and bruises from the struggle which had set them against each other, were often interlaced. Blood oozed from their noses and mouths; their faces, bloated and blue, were so deformed as to be almost unrecognizable. Nevertheless, some of the *Sonder-kommando* often did recognize their kin. The encounter was not easy, and I dreaded it for myself. I had no reason to be here, and yet I had come down among the dead. I felt it my duty to my people and to the entire world to be able to give an accurate account of what I had seen if ever, by some miraculous whim of fate, I should escape.[1]

[1] Dr Miklos Nyiszli, *Auschwitz* (Panther Books, 1962).

Hoess boasted that he knew of no one who had escaped the living death of the gas chambers. He was wrong. In Auschwitz, Dr Miklos Nyiszli describes how he found a frail 16-year-old girl naked and struggling for breath.

The chief of the gas chamber *kommando* almost tore the hinges off the door to my room as he arrived out of breath, his eyes wide with fear or surprise.

'Doctor,' he said, 'come quickly. We just found a girl alive at the bottom of the pile of corpses.'

I grabbed my instrument case, which was always ready, and dashed to the gas chamber. Against the wall, near the entrance of the immense room, half covered with other bodies, I saw a girl in the throes of a death-rattle, her body seized with convulsions. The gas *kommando* men around me were in a state of panic. Nothing like this had ever happened in the course of their horrible career.

We removed the still living body from the corpses pressing against it. I gathered the tiny adolescent body in my arms and carried it back into the room adjoining the gas chamber, where normally the gas *kommando* men change clothes for work. I laid the body on a bench. A frail young girl, almost a child, she could have been no more than 15. I took out my syringe and, taking her arm – she had not yet recovered consciousness and was breathing with difficulty – I administered three intravenous injections. My companions covered her body which was as cold as ice with a heavy overcoat. One ran to the kitchen to fetch some tea and warm broth. Everybody wanted to help, as if she were his own child.

The reaction was swift. The child was seized by a fit of coughing, which brought up a thick globule of phlegm from her lungs. She opened her eyes and looked fixedly at the ceiling. I kept a close watch for every sign of life. Her breathing became deeper and more and more regular. Her lungs, tortured by the gas, inhaled the fresh air avidly. Her pulse became perceptible, the result of the injections. I waited impatiently. The injections had not yet been completely absorbed, but I saw that within a few minutes she was going to regain consciousness: her circulation began to bring colour back into her cheeks, and her delicate face became human again.

She looked around her with astonishment, and glanced at us. She still did not realize what was happening to her, and was still incapable of distinguishing the present, of knowing whether she was dreaming or really awake. A veil of mist clouded her consciousness. Perhaps she vaguely remembered a train, a long line of box cars which had brought her here.

Then she had lined up for selection and, before she knew what was happening, been swept along by the current of the mass into a large, brilliantly lighted underground room. Everything had happened so quickly. Perhaps she remembered that everyone had had to undress. The impression had been disagreeable, but everybody had yielded resignedly to the order. And so, naked, she had been swept along into another room. Mute anguish had seized them all. The second room had also been lit by powerful lamps. Completely bewildered, she had let her gaze wander over the mass huddled there, but found none of her family. Pressed close against the wall, she had waited, her heart frozen, for what was going to happen. All of a sudden the lights had gone out, leaving her enveloped in total darkness. Something had stung her eyes, seized her throat, suffocated her. She had fainted. There her memories ceased.

Her movements were becoming more and more animated; she tried to move her hands, her feet, to turn her head left and right. Her face was seized by a fit of convulsions. Suddenly she grasped my coat collar and gripped it convulsively, trying with all her might to raise herself. I laid her back down again several times, but she continued to repeat the same gesture. Little by little, however, she grew calm and remained stretched out, completely exhausted. Large tears shone in her eyes and rolled down her cheeks. She was not crying. I received the first reply to my questions. Not wanting to tire her, I asked only a few. I learned that she was 16 years old, and that she had come with her parents in a convoy from Transylvania.

The *kommando* gave her a bowl of hot broth, which she drank voraciously. They kept bringing her all sorts of dishes, but I could not allow them to give her anything. I covered her to her head and told her that she should try and get some sleep.

My thoughts moved at a dizzy pace. I turned towards my companions in the hope of finding a solution. We racked our brains, for we were now face to face with the most difficult problem: what to do with the girl now that she had been restored to life? We knew that she could not remain here for very long.

What could one do with a young girl in the crematorium's *Sonderkommando*? I knew the past history of the place: no one had ever come out of here alive, either from the convoys or from the *Sonderkommando*.

Little time remained for reflection. *Oberschaaführer* Mussfeld arrived to supervise the work, as was his wont. Passing by the open door, he saw us gathered in a group. He came in and asked what was going on. Even before we told him he had seen the girl stretched out on the bench.

I made a sign for my companions to withdraw. I was going to attempt something. I knew without saying it was doomed to failure. Three months in the same camp and in the same milieu had created, in spite of everything, a certain intimacy between us. Besides, the Germans generally appreciate capable people, and, as long as they need them, respect them to a certain extent, even in the KZ. Such was the case for cobblers, tailors, joiners and locksmiths. From our numerous contacts, I had been able to ascertain that Mussfeld had a high esteem for the medical expert's professional qualities. He knew that my superior was Dr Mengele, the KZ's most dreaded figure, who, goaded by racial pride, took himself to be one of the most important representatives of German medical science. He considered the dispatch of hundreds of thousands of Jews to the gas chambers as a patriotic duty. The work carried on in the dissecting room was for the furtherance of German medical science. As Dr Mengele's pathological expert, I also had a hand in this progress, and therein lay the explanation for a certain form of respect that Mussfeld paid me. He often came to see me in the dissecting room, and we conversed on politics, the military situation and various other subjects. It appeared that his respect also arose from the fact that he considered the dissection of bodies and his bloody job of killing to be allied activities. He was the commandant and ace shot of number one crematorium. Three other SS acted as his lieutenants. Together they carried out the 'liquidation' by a bullet in the back of the neck. This type of death was reserved for those who had been chosen in the camp, or else sent from another on their way to a so-called 'rest camp'. When there were merely 500 or less, they were killed by a bullet in the back of the neck, for the large factory of gas chambers was reserved for the annihilation of more important numbers. As much gas was needed to kill 500 as to kill 1,000. Nor was it worthwhile to call out the Red Cross truck to bring the canisters and gas butchers for such a trifling number of victims. Nor was it worth the trouble of having a truck come to collect the clothes, which were scarcely more than rags anyway. Such were the factors which determined whether a group would die by gas or by a bullet in the back of the neck.

And this was the man I had to deal with, the man I had to talk into allowing a single life to be spared. I calmly related the terrible case we found ourselves confronted with. I described for his benefit what pains the child must have suffered in the undressing room, and the horrible scenes that preceded death in the gas chamber. When the room had been plunged into darkness, she had breathed in a few lungfuls of cyclon gas. Only a few, though, for her fragile body had given way under the pushing and shoving of the mass as they fought against death. By chance she had fallen with her face against the wet concrete floor. That bit of humidity had kept her from being asphyxiated, for cyclon gas does not react under humid conditions.

These were my arguments, and I asked him to do something for the child. He listened to me attentively, then asked me exactly what I proposed doing. I saw by his expression that I had put him face to face with a practically impossible problem. It was obvious that the child could not remain in the crematorium. One solution would have been to put her in front of the crematorium gate. A *kommando* of women always worked here. She could have slipped in among them and accompanied them back to the camp barracks after they had finished work. She would never relate what had happened to her. The presence of one new face among so many thousands would never be detected, for no one in the camp knew all the other inmates.

If she had been three or four years older that might have worked. A girl of 20 would have been able to understand clearly the miraculous circumstances of her survival, and have enough foresight not to tell anyone about them. She would wait for better times, like so many other thousands were waiting, to recount what she had lived through. But Mussfeld thought that a young girl of 16 would in all naiveté tell the first person she met where she had just come from, what she had seen and what she had lived through. The news would spread like wildfire, and we would all be forced to pay for it with our lives.

'There's no way of getting round it,' he said, 'the child will have to die.'

Half an hour later the young girl was led, or rather carried into the furnace room hallway, and there Mussfeld sent another in his place to do the job. A bullet in the back of the neck.[2]

² Ibid.

Eichmann's organizational skill and efficiency frequently caused logistical problems for the staff at Auschwitz and to alleviate things, the engineer Pruefer of the construction firm I.A. Topf & Sons was given the contract to construct an efficient and special crematorium at Auschwitz.

In his memoirs, Rudolf Hoess explains the problems of the old-style crematorium. 'During bad weather or when a strong wind was blowing, the stench of burning flesh was carried for many miles and caused the whole neighbourhood to talk about the burning of Jews, despite official counter-propaganda. Moreover the air defence services protested against the fires which could be seen from great distances at night.' Hoess continued, 'Nevertheless, burnings had to go on, even at night, unless further transports were to be refused.'

In comparing Auschwitz to other concentration camps, Hoess remarks that in Treblinka, for instance, the inefficient operation meant that the exhaust gases sometimes failed to do the job. He writes, 'Many of them were only rendered unconscious and had to be finished off by shooting.'

Hoess writes that the two large crematoria at Auschwitz, I and II, could cremate about 2,000 bodies in less than 24 hours. The smaller crematoria, III and IV, made by the construction firm of Topf of Erfurt, could burn about 1,500 bodies within 24 hours. Quoting statistics, he writes, 'The highest total number of people gassed and cremated within 24 hours was rather more than 9,000. This figure was attained in the summer of 1944, during the action in Hungary.'

Chapter 4
✦✦✦

EUROPE IS JEW-FREE ... ALMOST!

London, 1942

In August 1942, the Allies received evidence that Hitler had ordered the erection of enormous gas chambers to be used for the annihilation of Europe's Jews. Four months later, in December 1942, the Allies publicly admitted that the Jews of Europe were the targets for extermination.

In the House of Commons, British Foreign Secretary Anthony Eden stated, 'The Nazis are now carrying into effect Hitler's oft-repeated intention to exterminate the Jewish people of Europe.'

But what could be done to save them? During the last three years of the war, Jewish leaders proposed paying a ransom to release communities, to issue mass visas, and suggested bombing Auschwitz and the railway lines leading to the gas chambers.

Virtually all the proposals were rejected. Although sites within 10 kilometres of Auschwitz were bombed, no aircraft could be spared to destroy the crematoria and therefore slow down the rate of extermination.

Required to respond to the plight of the Jews in the light of the world's attention focused on Europe, the Allies settled on the inevitable, a conference. Set for January 1943 in Bermuda, the conference in effect completed the ceremony of public hand-washing.

By the time the meeting had ended, in April 1943, 3 million Jews were dead. The Nazi extermination camps were gassing and killing an average of 15,000 people a day.

Reporting on the Bermuda Conference, the London *Observer* noted:

> Here are the leisurely beach hotels of the Atlantic luxury island where well-dressed gentlemen assemble to assure each other in the best Geneva fashion that really nothing much can be done. The opening speeches of the conference have been widely noted in this country, and noted with dismay and anger. We have been told this problem is beyond the resources of Britain and America combined ... if they cannot help, who can? What is so terrible about these speeches is not only their utter insensitiveness to human suffering. It is the implied readiness of the two greatest powers on earth to humiliate themselves, to declare themselves bankrupt and impotent, in order to evade the slight discomfort of charity...

The conference itself ended in a dismal failure as far as solving the Jewish refugee problem was concerned. The Third Reich, however, was having no difficulty in carrying out its own solution to the problem.

The International Red Cross maintained that they could not interfere in internal affairs. The ceremony of the folded arms. Tight immigration restrictions imposed by the British and the Americans cut off further Jewish hopes of deliverance.

Although individual Christians hid Jewish friends, the Catholic Church in Germany uttered no protest and the Protestant Churches remained equally silent.

Martin Niemöller, an evangelical pastor, supported resistance to the Reich. For this stance, Niemöller and other Christian leaders were marched to the camps where many perished. In one of his memorable sermons, Niemöller challenged his congregation to take a stand for justice. It was the way of the cross, he insisted.

Attributed to him is the challenge, 'Then they came for the Jews, and I didn't speak up because I wasn't a Jew ... And when they came for the Catholics I didn't speak up, because I was a Protestant. Then they came for me ... And by that time there was no one left to speak for anyone...'

It was noted that the deportations of Jews were halted in states occupied by or allied to Germany when the Churches campaigned against such practices.

The Bulgarian Church actively supported Sofia's protection of its Jewish community and Bulgarian Jewry slipped through the net. The government halted the production of the yellow star by cutting off the electricity supply to the plant producing the badges.

Individuals in Sweden succeeded in smuggling more than 800 of Norway's Jews across the border to safety. In another daring rescue, virtually the entire Danish population hid several thousand Jews and successfully transported them by sea to Sweden, managing to avoid the German blockades.

A Gestapo report, dated 18 March 1942, detailed the activities of a Christian named Karl Golda, aged 28, a member of the Order of the Salesians, living in a monastery near Auschwitz. He investigated the camps and documented his findings. However, it was dangerous to display too much curiosity. He was arrested and sent to Auschwitz, where he perished on 14 May 1942. For Karl Golda, to remain silent was to strengthen the advocates of evil. His story remains an inspiring footnote to history.

Berlin

Hitler probably realized that the Allies were not going to save the Jews. One month after the Wannsee Conference, on 24 February 1942, the ship *Struma* with 769 Jewish refugees on board, having been refused permission by the British to enter Palestine and been forced back towards Bulgaria by the Turks, sank in the Bosphorus with the loss of all but one passenger.

When the ship *Salvador* sank in 1940 in the Sea of Marmara with the loss of 200 lives, the head of the British Foreign Office Refugee Department, T.M. Snow, wrote that he considered the event 'an opportune disaster'. One year earlier, the day before World War II began, on 2 September 1939, British patrols fired gunshots at the *Tiger Hill*, a refugee ship carrying 1,400 'illegal immigrants' to Palestine. The previous year, in 1938, when the US called an international conference in Evian to deal with the 'refugee problem', only one country was willing to offer a resettlement programme: the Dominican Republic. Australia declined to help, reasoning, 'We have no real racial problem. We are not desirous of importing one.'

Hitler had already observed the Free World's response to the Armenian genocide perpetrated by the Turks in 1915. Victims of an unprecedented annihilation by the Turkish invaders, more than 1.5 million Armenians were murdered in Turkish Armenia, and between 5 and 6 million Armenians were forced into exile, to be scattered throughout the world.

The Western world expressed outrage at the time of the mass murders. On 20 December 1917 Lloyd George, the British Prime Minister, described Armenia as a land soaked in the blood of the innocent, and the following year, in the summer of 1918, the Prime Minister again declared that Britain would never forget its responsibilities to the Armenians. In addition, the American President and several European leaders expressed sympathy and support for the Armenian cause.

Relying on such promises proved catastrophic for the Armenians, as the eventual Treaty of Lausanne, agreed in July 1923, largely ignored earlier commitments made by the Allies to the Armenians. Armenia disappeared from the map of the world and today few people remember that it was once an independent nation and one of the first to adopt Christianity as a religion.

Carefully observing the Allied response to the Armenians, Adolf Hitler remarked on 22 August 1939, 'I have given orders to my Death Units to exterminate without any mercy or pity men, women and children belonging to the Polish-speaking race. It is only in this manner that we can acquire the vital territory which we need. After all, who remembers today the extermination of the Armenians?'

Hitler perceived that once the impact of the deportations had subsided and slipped from public memory, it would give way to written outrage and far more dignified acts of protest and retaliation.

Understandably, Joseph Goebbels commented in his diary about the Allied reaction to the Final Solution, 'Fundamentally, however, I believe both the English and the Americans are happy that we are exterminating the Jewish riffraff.'

The pornography of genocide practised by Adolf Hitler and perpetrated by such men as Eichmann and Mengele came perilously close to fulfilling its objective of making Europe *Judenrein* – Jew-free.

In all, about 6 million Jews were destroyed. The number represents roughly one-third of the present Jewish population and is equivalent to those still alive in 1939. Of those numbers, about 5 million victims perished in the concentration camps and mass exterminations carried out in Europe.

By 1944, the collapse of the Third Reich seemed inevitable, the war almost over. With his back to the wall, Hitler refused to concede defeat or discuss withdrawals and escape. His mind raced with military strategies, yet he still found time to turn to his personal obsession, the Jews.

He was enraged by the situation in Hungary, his supposed ally, where somehow 900,000 Jews had evaded the camps, and in a moment of fury in March 1944 he sent the notorious Adolf Eichmann to take care of the business. With no one to stem the torrent, the fate of Hungarian Jewry seemed inevitable. The solution was final.

Almost…

Chapter 5

❖❖❖

THE TERRIBLE SECRET

London/Stockholm, 1942 – Washington, January 1944

Did the Allies know what was happening to the Jews of Europe, and could they have done more to rescue them? The question rises from the ashes to haunt our generation.

Recently uncovered memoranda from the Foreign Office archives betray a callous and cynical attitude among some officials. Perhaps they found it impossible to believe the incredible stories filtering through. However the memos, dictated, typed and disseminated along the corridors of Whitehall, formed British policy on the plight of European Jewry. In retrospect they make disturbing reading:

> 'Why should the Jews be spared distress and humiliation when they have earned it?' reads one minute. And another: 'In my opinion, a disproportionate amount of time of the Office is wasted on dealing with these wailing Jews.' And another: 'What is disturbing is the apparent readiness of the new Colonial Secretary to take Jewish Agency "sob stuff" at its face value.'[1]

The subject is scrutinized in Richard Breitman's book, *Official Secrets: What the Nazis Planned, What the British and Americans Knew.* The

[1] *The Listener,* 16 September 1982.

author presents newly declassified documents revealing that certain British officials had incontrovertible evidence of portions of the Holocaust 'directly from decodes of German police and SS messages'. Yet this critical evidence was sealed away – marked 'most secret', 'to be kept under lock and key' and 'never to be removed from this office'. It has only recently been released and Breitman's important book exposes British and American suppression of information about Nazi killings, as well as the tension between the two powers about how to respond.

Neutral Sweden also received first-hand accounts from a Swedish Colony in Warsaw. Later on, in August 1942, Swedish diplomat Baron von Otter was told of the death camps while travelling on the Warsaw–Berlin express. The train was packed with soldiers and refugees. Also on board was Kurt Gerstein, the SS's chief 'disinfection officer' who had helped develop and deliver the Cyclon B gas used in the mass murders.

Gerstein told von Otter that he had stepped into hell itself and related horror after horror. On one occasion, he had witnessed a mass killing where the gas release mechanism had failed. Gerstein timed the final moments of the bodies pressed together in the room of death. The agony lasted three hours. Gerstein showed von Otter his documentary evidence and urged the diplomat to tell the world. He felt people everywhere would revolt against the Nazis if only they knew. Historian Walter Laqueur, in *The Terrible Secret*, claims that the information was buried by Staffan Soderblom at the Swedish Foreign Ministry. Some years later Soderblom was to play a disastrous role in Raoul Wallenberg's future.

America's policy towards the Jews was changed by a report entitled *The Acquiescence of this Government in the Murder of the Jews* which was presented to President Roosevelt. The document charged that the American government had failed to halt Hitler's assault on the Jews and had prevented their rescue.

Within a week, Roosevelt established the War Refugee Board, on 22 January 1944, to aid the remnant of European Jewry, and responsibility for the task was placed on John Pehle, one of the original authors of the report. Within hours, Pehle moved into action, assisting those stranded in Europe with visas and safe passage, but also pressuring neutral powers, religious groups and relief organizations to help the Jews. The International Red Cross was also persuaded to improve its own policy on assistance.

If Pehle was pleased with his progress, he was not to know that within eight weeks of the Refugee Board's formation, it was to face its severest challenge.

In Berlin, Adolf Eichmann received his orders with elation and made immediate plans to leave for Hungary. Hitler invited the Hungarian regent, Admiral Miklos Horthy, for a two-day visit, from 17 to 19 March, to discuss the clearing up of the 'Jewish problem'. While Horthy maintained the pretence of power and independence, the reality of the situation unfolded. During his absence, 11 German divisions rolled into his homeland. Just hours after the coup, a mile-long special operations column motored into the capital city of Budapest. At its head was Adolf Eichmann.

Corralled in Hungary were the last survivors of Europe's Jews. He could hardly wait. Eichmann established his office in the Majestic Hotel on Buda's Suab Hill. When he assembled the Jewish community leaders in a large, ornate stateroom a few days later, he roared with laughter as he watched them sitting meekly before him. 'You know who I am, don't you?' he said. 'I am the one known as the bloodhound.'

Gestapo units combed the city, swooping on prominent Jews and anti-Nazis. They came well prepared with a hit list of key Jewish figures, including lawyers, politicians and businessmen. Journalists, doctors and lawyers were picked out of the telephone book and moved to makeshift internment camps. In all, 3,451 Jews were arrested.

A wave of suicides hit Budapest. A mood of despair hung over the city. The Nazi phenomenon that had brutalized Europe had finally knocked on Hungary's door. Here it was. *Occupation!*

Pehle began to focus the attention of the War Refugee Board on Hungary and appealed to Church leaders to help. The Pope took a month to reply. The International Red Cross confirmed their powerlessness to act. The situation, they said, was 'beyond our capabilities'. The Catholic Primate of Hungary interceded for baptized Jews. His appeals were rewarded. The SS instructed this group to wear a white cross to accompany the yellow star that every Jew was forced to wear. By the time the Pope sent a message to Horthy, the Hungarian regent, it was too late. The deportations to Auschwitz had claimed many lives.

Soon the American President himself was broadcasting messages directly into Hungary, warning those who collaborated with the Nazis that a day of reckoning was inevitable. Roosevelt urged support for the Jews, pleading, 'It would be tragic if those innocent people, who have already survived a decade of Hitler's fury, should perish on the very eve of the triumph over the barbarians.'

It is hard to tell whether Roosevelt's messages boosted the morale of Hungary's Jews. By 1944, Jews were forbidden from owning radios or listening to foreign radio broadcasts.

Two months after Eichmann's first meeting with the Jewish Council in Budapest, wide-eyed and nervous men, women and children climbed aboard cattle cars and carriages heading for Auschwitz.

'Pack them in like herrings!' Eichmann shouted as he stood at the railway station personally supervising the operation, which was undertaken by Hungarian gendarmes. About 80–100 people were jammed into each tiny boxcar. It is estimated that a tenth of these died before reaching the Hungarian border.

Each day between 10,000 and 12,000 Jews were shunted to the camps. The crematoria at Auschwitz were on overload and the mechanism of death went into a round-the-clock operation. Auschwitz's Commandant, Rudolf Hoess, increased the staffing required for the gassing from 200 men to 600. The gas chambers and ovens were operated day and night and Hungarian Jews still lined up at the gates of the death camp. At times, guards grabbed young Jewish children and pitched them, screaming insanely, onto huge bonfires.

Eichmann himself was at the station for the departure of the first death train on 5 May. By 13 June, a total of 147 trains had delivered 437,000 Hungarian Jews to Auschwitz and other camps.

In two months, Eichmann's skilled team had swept the Hungarian landscape clean of Jews. He told a colleague, 'It went like a dream.' In a report to Berlin, Eichmann reported, 'The complete liquidation of the Hungarian Jews is an accomplished fact. Technical details will only take a few more days in Budapest.'

Relaxing in the bar at the Arizona nightclub, Eichmann confided to close colleagues that he planned to round up the entire Jewish population of Budapest in a single day. It was a spectacular idea, the highlight of his career, and was scheduled for 6 July. Under considerable pressure, however, Horthy demanded a suspension of the deportation.

When Eichmann heard the news, he was outraged and screamed, 'In all my long practice this is the first time such a thing has happened. This won't do at all. I can't get over it!'

The Jews of Budapest stayed behind closed doors. When they had to venture out, they could be seen walking dejectedly through the streets before curfew. Just how long could the Hungarian regent resist the forcefulness of Eichmann?

Stockholm, June 1944

In Stockholm, Raoul Wallenberg remained an innocent bystander to unfolding events, unaware that he was about to be thrust into a web of intrigue and danger.

Raoul's business partner, the Hungarian Jew Koloman Lauer, had met an American diplomat working for the Office of Strategic Services (OSS), the forerunner of the Central Intelligence Agency (CIA). Iver Olsen told Lauer about the recently formed War Refugee Board and said that he wanted to recruit a Swedish national who could go to Hungary to rescue Jews. Lauer's immediate response was, 'I know just the man.' Lauer's parents-in-law were trapped in Hungary and Raoul had already offered to help. He was sure that his young friend would be interested in this new project.

Olsen was impressed with the illustrious Wallenberg name. Jacob Wallenberg had served as head of the Swedish trade delegation to Nazi Germany and had arranged for material to be supplied to the *Führer*'s war effort. Jacob also maintained contact with a group of conspirators who were planning Hitler's assassination and he became the main conduit for ferrying messages to the Allies and the British leader, Winston Churchill. On Hitler's instructions, the conspirators in the failed attempt on his life were hanged by piano wire from a row of butcher's hooks in 1944. The execution was filmed by a cameraman who recorded their final agonies for the *Führer*'s pleasure.

Meanwhile, Marcus Wallenberg, Raoul's other cousin, was heading a trade mission to Britain. The Wallenbergs were juggling business deals between Britain and Germany and somehow maintaining trade links with both. They dealt with iron ore, a commodity Germany urgently needed.

Lauer brought Raoul and Olsen together for dinner, but they stayed talking until five the next morning. The US diplomat was convinced that they had found the right man to represent the War Refugee Board. The meeting left Raoul exhausted but exhilarated.

Still more meetings followed and eventually he met the US Minister Johnson, who also shared Olsen's judgement about Raoul's appointment. Raoul was to be President Roosevelt's personal representative in Hungary, the only Swedish diplomat so assigned behind enemy lines for the purpose of rescuing Jews.

Raoul felt convinced that the mission would only succeed on his terms, and he drew up a nine-point memorandum. He wanted the authority to use every means possible and to have no bureaucratic ties whatsoever with the Swedish Embassy in Budapest. He should have exclusive diplomatic privileges, unlimited funds, deal directly with all government agencies, yet retain a legitimate diplomatic position at the Embassy.

The memo required two weeks of intense negotiations at the Foreign Office in Stockholm. His demands were raised with the Prime Minister and cleared by King Gustav V himself.

The Allied landings in Normandy on 6 June had been deemed a success and the war, it would seem, had taken a decisive turn against Germany. Although this did not alter Eichmann's plans, it may have influenced events in the Swedish Foreign Office. Be that as it may, Raoul's appointment was approved on 23 June and he made plans to leave for Budapest at the beginning of August. He would spend July clearing up his business affairs and saying goodbye to his friends.

Many of Raoul's friends expressed surprise that he was going to Hungary at such a dangerous moment in the war. His sympathy for the Jewish cause was known, however. He had told the Americans that he was half-Jewish. In fact, his maternal grandmother was one-quarter Jewish.

Viveca Lindfors, a vivacious young actress, dated Raoul following his return from Palestine. She recalled, 'He took me up to his grandfather's office and I thought he wanted to seduce me. Instead he started telling me, almost in whispers, what was happening to the Jews in Germany. I just didn't understand it. I didn't believe him. I thought he was trying to win my sympathy.'

With over a month still to go before his departure, Raoul undertook some research on current events in Hungary and visited the Foreign Office to read through official dispatches. Hunched over a desk in the Swedish ministry building, he was deeply stirred by the chilling reports. 'Dear God, help those people,' he whispered. 'Help me to help them...'

The reports proved compulsive reading and after his second day in the Foreign Office, Raoul could barely contain his restlessness. Unlike other civil servants who had read the same texts,

Raoul realized that Hungary's Jews were in great peril. Even as he sat in Stockholm turning the pages, several thousands of Hungarian Jews were being deported from Budapest. He told his business partner Kolomon Lauer, 'Every day counts. I must leave as soon as possible.'

At the time, Eichmann was sending 10–12,000 Jews a day to Auschwitz and certain death. Gripped by the tragedy, Raoul changed his plans and decided to leave at once. He set 6 July as the day for his departure.

On his last night in Stockholm the leaders of the Jewish community assembled to meet this 31-year-old volunteer diplomat. Rabbi Ehrenpreis had originally considered him too young for the assignment, but now bestowed on him a Talmudic blessing: 'Those who set off on a mission of humanity can be assured of God's special protection.'

Fritz Hollander, a businessman, was part of the gathering and in 1980 he told Elenore Lester, 'It was a solemn evening. We knew what had already happened and we knew he was going on a dangerous mission. But we had one thought – that his name would be a protection – the Germans wouldn't dare to harm a Wallenberg. We had no thought about the Russians.'

Raoul was clearly moved by the occasion. He rose slowly, thanked each one for coming and for their prayers. Then he said, 'It's late and I have yet to pack my clothes. I'm sorry, but I must leave now. Thank you, my friends...'

At the door, Rabbi Ehrenpreis embraced Raoul, overcome with the emotion of the moment. 'You are in the hands of God,' he said.

Early the following morning, Hollander and Lauer accompanied Raoul to Stockholm's Bromma airport, where he caught a flight to Berlin for a stopover with his half-sister, Nina. She was married to Gunnar Lagergren, an attaché with the Swedish Embassy in Berlin. Although pleased to see her brother, she was somewhat preoccupied with forthcoming events and with the birth of her first child, just two months away.

Assuming that Raoul would spend some time with his sister, the Swedish Ambassador had reserved a berth on the sleeper leaving for Budapest in two days' time. When Raoul learned that his journey was to be delayed, his frustration was evident. Nina recalled his words as follows: 'I would like to spend some time with you, but I cannot waste a moment. Forgive me, Nina, but I must leave on the first available train.'

After checking travel schedules, Raoul located a train leaving for Budapest the next morning. There would be no time for a reservation. It would have to do. That night, British bombers circled Berlin and the wailing sirens drove Raoul, Nina and Gunnar into an air-raid shelter for protection. After a sleepless night, Raoul kissed Nina tenderly and said, 'We'll get together soon and catch up on old times. The war can't last much longer. It'll soon be over and we'll all be together again at home with mother.' Pausing a moment, he continued, 'I'm going to be an uncle! Great news! Let me know as soon as the baby is born.'

After waving goodbye, he was driven to Berlin's Anhatter Bahnhof where the Budapest express was waiting at the platform. The train was packed with soldiers in uniforms and weary travellers fleeing the war. Raoul bought a one-way ticket to Budapest and climbed on board. He spent the journey sitting on his rucksack in the crowded corridor of the train. His baggage resembled an adventurer's rather than a diplomat's: two bulging rucksacks and a sleeping bag. Carefully concealed amongst his possessions were crumpled bits of paper with names and addresses of key contacts in Budapest. Some were corrupt Hungarian officials who could be bribed, others were members of the underground. He also carried messages for Jewish families in Budapest and a list of Hungarian Jews of special interest to the Americans.

As the train pulled out of Berlin, he caught a glimpse of his reflection in the train window – his hat pulled low over his face, long black leather coat, hiking boots. 'I look more like a spy than a diplomat!' he thought to himself, somewhat amused at the notion that he could be mistaken for either.

He reached into his coat pocket and traced with his fingers the small revolver that he had purchased second-hand. Later he told a friend, 'I don't intend to use it. It's just there to give me courage.'

The passenger train that rolled into Budapest on 9 July 1944, with a weary Raoul Wallenberg on board, probably passed *en route* another train of 29 sealed cattle cars bound for Auschwitz. Inside the compartments, Jews from the Hungarian countryside completed what Eichmann proudly called 'a deportation surpassing every preceding deportation in magnitude'.

With typical German precision, Eichmann could report that between 14 May and 8 July, 437,402 Jewish men, women and children had been transported to Auschwitz aboard 148 trains.

Chapter 6

❖

RAOUL IN BUDAPEST

Budapest, July 1944

The dark green taxi stopped directly outside the Swedish Legation's office, high on Gelbert Hill in Buda. Raoul paid the driver and, clutching his rucksacks, headed unsteadily for the gate. All along the street, a solemn group of men and women queued, each clutching papers and files. The yellow star on their outer coats revealed their identity.

'Excuse me,' he said and shuffled on inside the building. The minister in charge of the Legation, Ivan Danielsson, had been alerted and Raoul was introduced to other officials. He was seated in one of the Legation's rooms, and a secretary brought him a steaming hot cup of coffee.

There was a tap on the door and a blond, well-dressed man entered the room. It was Per Anger. They had met before and hit it off well. Raoul would become a close friend and share many experiences with him in the days ahead.

'Welcome to Budapest!' Anger exclaimed. 'We didn't expect you so soon, but I'm glad you're here...' Raoul acknowledged the greeting and followed his gaze. Anger was too polite to say so, but the rucksacks and sleeping bag were hardly standard equipment for an ambitious young diplomat.

'Well, you know how it is these days,' Raoul joked, as he started to unwind from the journey. 'Tell me, who are those people at the gate? What do they want?'

Anger hesitated. 'You look tired and I'm sure you want a good hot bath first. Besides, I'm sure you have a lot more questions.'

Raoul smiled. 'I'm tired, it's true, but I can't wait to get started. Tell me. Tell me everything.'

Anger observed that he looked weak, timid and unimpressive. His receding hairline, slim build and shy, unassuming manner seemed ill-matched for the tough, aggressive Nazis and the local fascist thugs who were terrorizing the Jewish community. Still, Anger perceived Raoul's sense of urgency and intensity. He rose from his chair. 'Yes. OK, Raoul, I'll tell you what I know – but first let's get some more coffee and I'll order some sandwiches.'

Raoul Wallenberg was aware that he had stepped into a dangerous gutter of history. The Nazis were a law unto themselves and respected no authority but their own. Their test of a country's loyalty was the way they treated Jews. Hungary's ruling regent, Miklos Horthy, was losing his grip, aware that under his control the country was succumbing to Hitler's influence. All around, ruthless young politicians were planning coups to overthrow the government, forcing Hungary into the all-encompassing arms of the Third Reich. The main threat came from the Hungarian Nazi Party, an extreme fascist group called the Arrow Cross, who had modelled themselves on the German original. Stories of intrigue and political manoeuvrings seemed to dominate every conversation.

Wallenberg learned that the independent missions such as the Swedish and Swiss Legations were being squeezed out by a door that was swinging shut. There was little they could do.

The Jews made easy targets – the yellow star that they were forced to wear made them unmistakable. This was not the moment to be a friendly neighbour.

Wallenberg had an idea, however. During his first debriefing with Per Anger, and further conversations with people in the city, he learned that a 'letter of protection' issued by the Swedish Red Cross had enabled several hundred Jews to escape the dragnet. Convents and Christian missions had also sheltered a few children. The word on the street was that anyone with Swedish connections or travel plans was entitled to a provisional passport from the Legation, and 700 Jews had applied successfully for this document.

Wilhelm Forgas, one of the 700 Jews with a Swedish passport, had been rounded up and placed in a forced labour colony awaiting deportation to the death camps. Forgas plucked up courage one morning and showed his Swedish passport to a German officer on duty, who appeared flustered and eager to act correctly. He moved Forgas to an internment camp and the Swedish Legation got him out.

Another passport holder, Hugo Wohl, a former industrialist, hired a lawyer who championed his case through the courts. Wohl contended that he should be exempted from wearing a yellow star on his clothes and not be required to live in a yellow star house. Wohl won a significant victory and his case made legal history.

Wallenberg's imagination was captured by both accounts and he scrutinized each detail of the legal case in his office at the Swedish Legation. He found it astounding that an official document could halt the machine of death. He just could not get over it and kept pacing the floor, repeating the story to a group of aides in the room, marvelling at the impact of the psychology of bureaucracy.

He moved back to his desk, absorbed and preoccupied. 'What we need,' he told his colleagues, 'is an official-looking document that looks like a protective passport or *Schutzpass*. The design should be impressive and carry the personal signature of someone at the Embassy. It should also contain the Swedish emblem, in colour, if possible.'

He scribbled notes and produced some rough sketches while continuing to talk. 'It should also include a photograph of the passport holder, just like a real passport. It will look as though they are travelling to Sweden and in the meantime they are under our control.'

Someone in the office asked, 'But will Minister Danielsson agree to all this? After all, it's not entirely true, is it?'

'You leave that to me,' Raoul replied. 'I'll convince him. I'm more concerned that the passport convinces the Nazis. It's the psychological impact of the official document that will persuade the SS guards.'

Raoul contacted Forgas and Wohl, the enterprising Jews who had used the legality of bureaucracy to beat the Nazi system, and invited them to join his newly formed 'Section C' at the Swedish Legation. 'You're just the kind of men we need,' he told them. After designing the *Schutzpass* himself, he gave his new recruits their first assignment: to find a printer for the document.

The *Schutzpass* was a stroke of genius and a turning point for Wallenberg. If anyone was in doubt about his seriousness and suitability, here was the evidence.

He had observed that many of the Nazi soldiers and Hungarian thugs were poorly educated young men who would be impressed with an official-looking document. Raoul also used the power of propaganda by printing huge posters of the newly designed *Schutzpass* and placing them on billboards throughout the city. The signs proclaimed the authenticity of the document, guaranteeing the holder all the protective rights of a Swedish citizen. These advertising posters were designed to familiarize the Nazis with the document's authenticity.

The *Schutzpass* was signed by both Minister Danielsson and Wallenberg, and at first just 1,500 of these passports were printed. By wheeling and dealing, Raoul was able to get the quota increased. When fakes began to appear through the Jewish underground, he turned a blind eye. Through his influence, the *Schutzpass* was accepted as a legal document, even though it was actually a sham with no standing in international law.

Raoul's 'Section C' was born overnight, but, as one eyewitness recalled, 'within a week was so expertly run that it appeared to have been in place for at least a year'. The money raised by the War

Refugee Board was supplemented by wealthy Jewish families and Jewish organizations in Budapest. Raoul assembled a handpicked staff for 'Section C'. Within a few days more than 40 people were occupying three buildings and several automobiles had been purchased from Jewish businessmen for the venture. The reception area had several people to deal with enquiries and hand out application forms. Chairs, desks, filing cabinets and typewriters formed a bustling, busy office dedicated to producing and distributing the *Schutzpass*.

Raoul visited the Jewish Council's office at 12 Sip Street and handed over the letter of introduction from the Swedish Rabbi. He met the Council's chairman, Samu Stern, and other community leaders who sat solemn-faced before this somewhat naive young aristocrat who told them he was on their side.

What hope did he offer against the power of the Reich and the wrath of Eichmann? It was one man against the storm.

'Thank you, thank you,' one of the Jewish Council members replied politely after listening to Raoul's expression of solidarity.

In the office, Raoul met Dr Peto and his son, Laszlo, a childhood acquaintance whom he had first known at a summer camp at Lake Geneva. They were to share many experiences with Raoul during the next few months and Laszlo would occupy a special place in history as the last man ever to see Raoul Wallenberg in Budapest.

Raoul's first rescue mission ended in failure. During his first few days in Budapest, he rambled through the back streets to one of the addresses he had memorized back in Stockholm.

Kolomon Lauer, his partner in Sweden, had asked him to contact his wife's family in Budapest and Raoul had agreed. When he eventually located the address and knocked on their door, however, he learned that the family had been deported by the Nazis. It was his first acute disappointment. If only he had got there sooner...

In his first communication back to Sweden via the diplomatic pouch, he enclosed a note to his mother. 'Please invite the Lauers to the house,' he wrote. 'I don't dare tell them that Marika's parents and a small child in the family have certainly died during one of the deportations. I haven't the heart to tell him.'

The visit left him morose and dejected — not least because he was soon to learn the full implications of the relatively innocuous term 'deportation' and the full horror of the death camps.

One week after his arrival in Budapest, Wallenberg had picked up a document which contained eyewitness accounts of the killing machine at Auschwitz. Known as the 'Auschwitz Protocols', the document had been smuggled out of the camps by five prisoners who had escaped.

In Raoul's hands, the 'Auschwitz Protocols' made electrifying reading. On 18 July he cabled an extract to the Swedish Foreign Office in Stockholm as part of his first report home. The report detailed the crematoria working round the clock, gassing all those who stepped naked into the chamber. It told of the castration of men and the orchestra which was compelled to play popular waltzes to drown out the screams of innocent victims who were executed in groups of 200–300 after having been forced to dig their own graves.

The publication of the 'Auschwitz Protocols' around the world caused a sensation and led to the deportations being halted in Hungary.

Raoul had requested a meeting with the Hungarian regent, Miklos Horthy, and this was granted early in August. Raoul was undaunted by the occasion, or by the impressive Royal Palace, high on Buda Hill. He knew he would only have one moment to make his mark and he did not want to waste that opportunity. He was aware that the regent was under pressure to hand over Hungary's Jews to Eichmann and warned the elderly official that the Allies would not forget such an act. There would be a day of reckoning, the young diplomat ventured. The meeting was brief and Wallenberg was unceremoniously dismissed.

'He is an imposing figure,' Raoul told his colleagues back at the Legation, 'but during my meeting I felt morally taller than him.'

Raoul insisted on using his influence and learned never to waste an opportunity. At the Ministry of the Interior, he cajoled and bribed his way through a maze of red tape and prejudice. He was persistent, argumentative and resourceful. Backed into a corner, he could produce a bankroll bigger than his fist. He generally got what he wanted.

Through every means possible, he increased the quota of the *Schutzpass* from the initial 1,500 to 2,500, but was dissatisfied and returned to the Hungarian Ministry for another round of 'negotiations'. In exasperation, and worn out by his persistence, the officials at the Ministry succumbed and stretched the quota to include another 500 (eventually it reached 4,500), assuming that they had now seen the last of this crazy Swede.

The very next day Raoul returned with further demands.

'My staff are occupied with official business on behalf of the Swedish government,' he argued. 'I cannot see why they should be bothered with such formalities as wearing a yellow star on their clothes. This hinders our work, you know. I demand that they be given special permission and excused from this requirement.'

The argument continued relentlessly. When the weary Hungarian official explained that it was now civil law that all Jews should obey this command, Raoul countered, 'But this means my staff will only be permitted out on the streets for a few hours of the day. This hinders the official duties of the Royal Swedish government.' He then adopted a stern voice. 'Of course, you realize that I'll have to report this obstruction to my government.'

The debate continued. Raoul's stamina and inventiveness were the dominant factors. 'If you cannot give me an answer,' he said as he rose ominously to his feet, 'I'll just have to take it up with the regent himself. I didn't really want to bother him with such a trivial matter, but it'll have to be done. You leave me no option.' It may have been high farce, but as he was acting in the guise of a senior diplomat, the tactic secured a major victory.

The official was beaten. 'Mr Wallenberg, you are an expert negotiator,' he said. 'We will exempt your staff from wearing the badge. We are keen to be co-operative with your government. I hope you are pleased.' He rose to his feet, somewhat relieved that the contest was over. Did it really matter if a few Jews did not wear the yellow star?

Raoul, however, sat down again and leaned forward in his chair, ever the anxious politician. 'Minister, I'm pleased to hear this,' he said, 'but what about the other demands of the Swedish government?'

The minister appeared flustered, genuinely unaware of any other requests. 'But ... what do you mean? *Other* demands? What are you talking about?'

This time Raoul allowed himself to look perplexed. 'Haven't your assistants briefed you properly?'

'Well, yes, they have. They told me you were ... very persuasive in your arguments, and they told me about your staff's difficulties because of the yellow star they were forced to wear. That's all we can do. What else did you want?'

Now Raoul was at ease, circling the target, taking his time. 'Well, as I explained, what I want, and what the Swedish government demands, is that my staff be permitted to live in their own homes and not be moved into the "Jew houses".'

The minister looked truly puzzled. Seizing the moment, Raoul mounted an impressive and complex argument outlining the critical need for his staff to remain in their own homes and not be moved into specially marked houses for Jews. It was a gamble, but he was playing to win. Raoul concluded, 'As I explained, my government demands this. I hope you'll agree with me.'

The minister shuffled the papers on his desk. Leaning back in his chair, he appeared uncertain as to his next move. Without waiting, Raoul launched another salvo. If he were to report back to his Foreign Office, he mused, the Swedish government would have no option but to make an official complaint. Who knows where this might lead? Perhaps the minister himself would be blamed…

Sensing a breakthrough, Raoul dangled the bait. If we could clear this simple matter up quickly – it was, after all, a meagre concession – the minister could well find himself amply rewarded.

The hint was enough.

Wallenberg had won a second major victory. His staff, all Jews, were exempted from wearing the yellow star, which restricted their movements around the city and made them easy prey. They had also escaped from being herded into the ghetto.

Equally significant was the fact that Raoul had established his credibility and shown himself to be a person of formidable force who would stop at nothing to attain his objective.

However, his brash style was causing shock waves inside the Swedish Legation. Was this how a Swedish diplomat should behave? The showdown was inevitable and Raoul was summoned to Minister Danielsson's office to face a deluge of questions.

Lars Berg, an attaché at the Legation, recalls that these some-times painful discussions would last several hours. 'But in the end, Wallenberg always won. He won partly because he was so persistent, but finally because he had this very strong argument – it will save lives.'

It had been a whirlwind few weeks. Raoul had thrown himself into his assignment with zeal and dedication. Beyond his personal involvement, he proved that he had his finger on the pulse. What had begun as an adventure had turned into a mission. He seemed to be everywhere at once and his commission from God encom-passed everyone.

After listening to overseas radio broadcasts to Hungary, he cabled the Foreign Office: 'They only threaten those responsible for complicity in anti-Semite actions with harsh judgements for war crimes. They should also make offers of clemency and encourage a change in the present attitude.'

In one of his early reports to Stockholm, in July, he wrote, 'It is necessary to rouse the Jews from their apathy. We must get rid of their feeling that they have been abandoned.'

Chapter 7

❖❖❖

THE SAVING SCHUTZPASS

Budapest, August 1944

The Wallenberg passport, the *Schutzpass*, had created a stir throughout Budapest. The central post office was under siege as Jews ferreted through the Stockholm telephone directory for names and addresses of unknown Swedes who might possibly be able to offer any scrap of help.

All that was required to obtain a *Schutzpass* was to establish a link – anything – between themselves and someone in Sweden. Not surprisingly, a few days later the Stockholm directory was removed from the post office.

The *Schutzpass* boosted the morale of those Jews who received them. 'They made us somehow feel like human beings again,' Edit Emster asserted.

Of course, only a small portion of the Jewish community could be given the passes. There were about 175,000 Jews in Budapest and Raoul had secured permission to distribute 4,500 protective passes. Obviously, some criteria had to be established.

Wallenberg's 'Section C' was under siege. Each day the queue for *Schutzpass* application forms increased. In his office, Raoul was torn between handing out the passes to everyone and being more selective. He knew the effectiveness of the *Schutzpass* relied on its credibility if it was to save any Jews at all. By the middle of August, 20,000 Jews had applied for a *Schutzpass*, but still only 4,500 were available.

One evening, as Raoul stepped out of his Minerva Street office, he saw a woman sobbing helplessly by the side of the gate. She clutched a child in her arms, while a younger boy stood hesitantly at her side.

Raoul walked over and placed a comforting arm around her. 'Is there anything I can do for you?' he asked the woman, after offering her his handkerchief to dry her tears.

The woman explained that someone inside the building was handing out 'saving passes'. She had been coming to this gate every day for a week, but feared she would never reach the front of the queue. Every day, there seemed to be more and more people.

Raoul looked at her for a few moments. How could he walk away, leaving her crumpled and broken on the pavement? He helped her to her feet and asked her to wait. The woman never knew who he was, but she obeyed. He returned 15 minutes later and handed her a sealed brown envelope. Inside it was a life-saving *Schutzpass*.

Within a month, Wallenberg's operation had exploded. He moved 'Section C' out of the Swedish Legation and into two adjacent buildings. The unlimited supply of funds was used to set up a soup kitchen and two hospitals, with 40 physicians employed to work there. An underground press was kept busy printing *Schutzpasses* and other documents. At first about 250 workers were signed up; later that figure swelled to about 400, some working day and night alongside the Swedish diplomat. Many were key people picked specifically to handle what was now a vast operation. Others joined the Wallenberg network, after they were rescued personally by him from the clutches of the SS.

Wallenberg was not cut out to be a traditional diplomat, remote and inaccessible. Instead, he was practical and pragmatic; someone who would roll up his sleeves and join the team. He appeared controversial at times, but eventually inspired others to follow his example. The other neutral Embassies in Budapest — representing Spain, Portugal, Switzerland, El Salvador and the

Vatican – also issued protective passes and several neutral diplomats became involved in the plight of the Jews following Raoul's initiative. The Swiss protective passes proved popular and were widely distributed, but the *Schutzpass* issued by the Swedish 'Section C' proved most effective. It looked impressive, being printed in two colours, it carried a photograph of the holder, and it was personally signed by the Swedish Minister and Wallenberg. Most importantly, it was supported by Wallenberg's personal and persistent lobbying.

The passes became a source of grim humour. Often, when an Orthodox Jew strolled by on the street, dressed in his traditional hat, long beard and side-locks, his friends would call out, 'Look, there goes another Swede!'

Wallenberg seemed unstoppable. His latest move was equally dynamic and inventive. Aware that Jews were being picked up in the streets by armed gangs and that Jewish homes made easy targets, he launched the brilliant idea of protective houses for those with protective papers, whom he called 'International Jews'.

From his network of informants, Wallenberg learned that the Nazis were enraged by the suspension of the deportations and that they planned a fresh onslaught in the next few days.

Colonel Laszlo Ferenczy was a pivotal figure in Hungary. Under German occupation he had earned himself a reputation, working alongside SS men with great efficiency, carrying out the deportations of Jews from the Hungarian countryside to the camp at Auschwitz. Since the uneasy calm had fallen, he was the official liaison between Eichmann and the Hungarian government.

Only one man could grant Wallenberg permission for the 'International Jews' to be held in protective houses: Colonel Ferenczy.

As Raoul spoke no Hungarian, he invited Mrs Elizabeth Kasser, a voluntary worker for the Hungarian Red Cross, to accompany him as his interpreter, along with her husband Alexander. Years later, she recalled the incident.

Wallenberg, she stated, was furious as they were kept waiting for a long time in an anteroom of the Colonel's office. 'Finally Ferenczy came to us and made a long speech about how we should be ashamed of ourselves for helping Jews and what awful people Jews were,' she recalled.

After persistent negotiation, however, Wallenberg got his way. Ferenczy granted permission for three houses to be opened under special Swedish protection. They were to house 650 people who were to emigrate to Sweden as soon as circumstances allowed. Now in a good mood, Ferenczy also gave permission for the Swedish Red Cross to have similar houses.

'As soon as we were out of sight of that building,' Mrs Kasser said, 'we put our arms around each other and did a sort of Indian rain dance on the street.'

The Swedish safe houses marked the beginning of what was to be known as the 'international ghetto'. Over 30,000 Jews holding foreign passes would cram into these protected houses hoping to escape.

Wallenberg returned from the meeting to his office on Minerva Street and instructed an assistant to construct large Swedish flags which were to be hung outside the protected houses alongside the Jewish star. Eventually Wallenberg purchased 30 buildings to be used as schools, hospitals, soup kitchens and shelters for 5,000 children whose parents had already been deported or killed.

Following this initiative, the International Red Cross and other neutral Embassies also pressed for protected houses. After the war, about 25,000 Jews were found alive in the international ghetto; all were directly under Wallenberg's protection.

Officials at the Swedish Legation were not impressed with Wallenberg's style of diplomacy and were less than enthusiastic about some of his schemes. Iver Olsen of the US War Refugee Board, who had originally backed Wallenberg for the assignment, was drawn into the dilemma. He cabled Washington: 'I am of the impression that the Swedish Foreign Ministry are somewhat disturbed over Wallenberg's activities in Budapest, and they probably feel that he "jumped in with too big a splash". I am sure they would prefer he had dealt with the Jewish problem along traditional diplomatic lines, which would mean not helping the Jews.'

Eichmann and the Hungarian regent, under pressure from the Allies, were playing a tug-of-war game with the remaining Jews still living in Budapest. A new date for the deportations was set — 5 August, one day after Raoul's thirty-second birthday.

Horthy studied the situation carefully. Germany were in a precarious position and the war was going badly for them. The Russian army's recent advance brought them nearer Hungary with every offensive. Horthy's tactical move was to dismiss his Interior Minister, Andor Jaross, along with some of his aides. Horthy controlled the local gendarmes and without them there could be no deportations. Eichmann eased the loss with bouts of drinking at the Arizona nightclub and nights of debauchery at the Majestic Hotel. He had been outmanoeuvred. For the moment.

Throughout August Horthy rocked back and forth, trying to stabilize his cabinet and resist pressure from the Nazis. Horthy hoped to reach an armistice with Churchill and Roosevelt. As the war seemed to have swung decisively in favour of the Allies, the Hungarian regent was eager to appease them.

Not to be outdone, however, Eichmann set a new date for the deportations — 25 August — but Colonel Ferenczy leaked the news to Wallenberg and the Jewish leaders. Wallenberg immediately organized an official protest to the Prime Minister. The intervention had come at a strategic moment.

On 24 August, the day before the deportations, Romania surrendered to the Russians and declared war on Hungary and Germany. This left Hungary's southern border open, convincing Horthy that the war was lost. He immediately cancelled the deportations. On the same day, Himmler cabled Eichmann from Berlin, also ordering the cessation of the deportations.

Eichmann was a defeated man. He began preparations to leave Budapest and moved to the castle of Velem, near the Austrian border.

Horthy formed a new government and excluded the extreme Nazi faction, the Arrow Cross. By mid-September there were fewer than 450 Jews in internment camps and these were now under Horthy's care. The Jews of Budapest disregarded the curfew and took to appearing freely in the streets.

Wallenberg relaxed his efforts and wound down his operation, cutting his staff back to about 100 employees. He could reflect upon his assignment with a sense of accomplishment. In what is apparently a final report from Budapest, he wrote to Iver Olsen:

When I now look back on the three months I have spent here I can only say that it has been a most interesting experience, and I believe not without results. When I arrived the situation of the Jews was very bad indeed. The development of military events and a natural psychological reaction among the Hungarian people have changed many things. We at the Swedish Legation have perhaps only been an instrument to convert this outside influence into action in the various government offices. I have taken quite a strong line in this respect, although of course I have had to keep within the limits assigned to me as a neutral.

It has been my object all the time to try to help all Jews. This, however, could only be achieved by helping a whole group of Jews to get rid of their stars. I have worked on the hypothesis that those who were no longer under the obligation to wear the star would help their fellow-sufferers. Also I have carried out a great deal of enlightenment work among the key men in charge of Jewish questions here. I am quite sure that our activity – and that means in the last instance yours – is responsible for the freeing at this time of the interned Jews. These numbered many hundreds...

Mr Olsen, believe me, your donation on behalf of the Hungarian Jews has done an enormous amount of good. I think that they will have every reason to thank you for having initiated and supported the Swedish Jewish action the way you have in such a splendid manner.'

Raoul believed his work in Hungary was at an end, as the Russian army would soon be in the country. His thoughts returned to his own chequered career and his immediate future in Stockholm. He wrote to his friend and partner, Kolomon Lauer, requesting that he contact his cousin Jacob Wallenberg to enquire if a position within the Wallenberg empire could be found for him upon his return.

'I'll try to be home several days before the Russians arrive in Budapest,' he wrote to his family.

With one eye on the horizon, Raoul still kept in touch with routine affairs in the city. He believed these were his final days in Budapest. He negotiated a longer curfew for Jews, from 8 a.m. to 8 p.m., and obtained permission to reopen the synagogue. He also sought the release of Jews detained in Gestapo prisons.

' Swedish Foreign Office White Books on Raoul Wallenberg (Swedish Foreign Ministry, Stockholm, 1980).

Chapter 8

❥❥❥

RESCUE MISSION

Budapest, 15 October 1944

Like all the neutral diplomats, Raoul Wallenberg had heard the whispers. A special envoy from the Hungarian government had been sent secretly to Moscow to negotiate the terms of Horthy's surrender. With the Red Army just 50 miles south of Budapest, Horthy's bargaining power carried little weight and he agreed to announce his withdrawal on 18 October. On 10 October, however, a Hungarian army general was kidnapped in Budapest. Fearing a coup, Horthy stepped up his timetable and decided to announce his armistice with the Russians three days earlier than planned, on 15 October.

Around midday on the 15th, Wallenberg and almost everyone else in Budapest turned the dial on their wireless to hear the regent's statement about the end of the war. His speech was received with jubilation. All the horrors of recent days were blamed on the Gestapo and the SS. Things would be different, now that the war was over.

All over the city, doors were flung open and people poured into the streets to celebrate. Jews ripped the yellow stars from their clothes and tore them in half, throwing them into the street. Some lit bonfires.

Suddenly the radio was silent. Then music replaced the announcement of the armistice. German marches. Then another voice could be heard. Smiles turned to horror. The dreaded Arrow Cross had seized power. The Arrow Cross was a violent fascist group that had been launched as an imitation of the Nazi Party. Ferenc Szalasi, their leader, was taking charge. Within hours, the Nazis and Arrow Cross took command over strategic points in the city.

The news was confirmed through Wallenberg's network of informants. The word was that the Swedish diplomat paid for all kinds of news, both good and bad. One informant explained that Horthy's son had been kidnapped and was in German hands, forcing the aged regent into submission. The following day Horthy was escorted into exile in Germany and his son was deported to Mauthausen concentration camp.

Wallenberg received the news with surprise and alarm. This signalled the end of law and order.

Szalasi's coup was accompanied by a vicious campaign of terror. The Jews were the target. Teenage fascists armed with automatic rifles, machine guns and grenades cruised the streets, shooting Jews on sight. Dead bodies lay in the street where they had been slain.

A terrifying sight was the notorious Father Andras Kun, dressed in a flowing black cassock, brandishing a huge crucifix in one hand and a revolver in the other as he led a band of thugs through the streets. Jewish men and women were grabbed by his gang, beaten up, tortured and then dragged back to be shot in the street and dumped into the Danube.

A fresh wave of Jewish suicides swept Budapest as fear gripped the city once more. Jewish homes marked with yellow stars were sealed. The sick lay untended, the dead were unburied, and many starved. Christians hid some Jews, but risked being reported to the authorities and sharing the same deadly fate as their friends.

The next morning an uneasy lull hung over the city. Debris from the previous night's terror lay all around. Corpses floated down the Danube and dead bodies lay unclaimed in the streets where they had been slain. Faces peered through windows, as few people dared to venture out.

Raoul felt an October chill as he walked into his office and waited for his staff to arrive. No one turned up for work. Fearful of the gangs, many had gone into hiding. Raoul paced up and down the entrance to the office, peering down Gelbert Hill. It was clear no one was coming. Determined that his staff should not be intimidated, he decided to take the initiative. With no transportation, he borrowed a ladies' bicycle and started calling on the homes of those he knew.

'Trust me,' he told them. 'I'll protect you. I'll be there.'

Almost all of them accepted his invitation and returned to work. His rescue mission was now operating around the clock, and he managed to assemble around 400 volunteers. During times of extreme danger, most took shelter in the office, staying with Raoul while the fighting raged outside.

Raoul's earlier success in gaining exemption for his staff from wearing the yellow star was particularly valuable. They could now move around the city with a certain degree of freedom and impunity. The Arrow Cross had already murdered 300 Jews and the death toll was still to rise during the first 12 hours of Szalasi's coup.

While Raoul was pedalling around Budapest on a borrowed bicycle, a running gun battle had broken out in the heart of the ghetto. Jewish resistance fighters joined by a group of communists put up a brave fight in Teleki Square, but they were outnumbered by the SS men and Hungarian police, and they did not stand a chance. Within hours the square was littered with dead bodies. In swift retribution for daring to oppose them, the Arrow Cross dragged women and children from yellow star houses nearby and executed them in the square.

Raoul returned to his office that afternoon sweating from his cycling expedition. Already several of his staff were back.

'Has Vilmos returned?' Raoul questioned one of the other drivers whom he saw in the hallway of the building.

'No,' replied Sandor Ardai, one of the young Jewish men rescued by Wallenberg who now worked as a driver for 'Section C'.

Sandor continued, 'We heard that Vilmos has been arrested by the Arrow Cross and that your car has been confiscated.'

Raoul stared at Sandor, truly shocked by the news. Almost everyone in the office had a relative or a friend who was missing. Now Vilmos.

Vilmos Langfelder was a young Hungarian Jew who served as his chauffeur. He was an engineer from a prominent family of Jewish industrialists and, like many of Raoul's staff, had been rescued from one of the deportations. The two men were roughly the same age and both shared the same aloof, reserved temperament.

The news of Vilmos's arrest spurred Raoul into action. 'Do you know where Vilmos is being held?' he asked, the words spilling out as quickly as his thoughts.

'I'll find out,' Sandor replied. He walked down the corridor, leaving Raoul alone and wondering if he would ever see his driver again.

Sandor returned a short while later and saw Raoul dictating a letter of protest to the new government, threatening to break off diplomatic relations unless the terror stopped. He told Raoul that Vilmos was among others arrested and held in a jail at the Arrow Cross headquarters.

'It may not be too late,' Raoul said mysteriously, a flicker of hope in his eyes. He finished dictating his protest letter and then asked Sandor to drive him to the Arrow Cross building.

Sandor Ardai was nervous. This Swedish diplomat looked 'dreamy and weak'. Wallenberg was just one man, alone, unarmed and insignificant. What hope did he have of rescuing a single person? What did he expect? A miracle? Sandor kept these thoughts to himself as he drove Raoul through the streets of Budapest. Within moments the Swedish diplomat's car pulled up outside a grey building.

'Wait for me,' Wallenberg said as he left the car. Sandor was silent, staring at the Swede in his leather coat as he walked into the fascist headquarters. Outside, youths with machine guns lounged by the gates, boasting of the previous night's exploits – old men frightened to death, young girls sexually assaulted.

Half an hour later, Sandor Ardai could scarcely believe his eyes as he watched Raoul Wallenberg return to the car with Vilmos Langfelder. Somehow Wallenberg had worked a miracle. If there was a God who cared amidst this horror, he pondered to himself, then this was the evidence.

Sandor Ardai was beaming. He turned to Wallenberg, a fresh respect and admiration in his eyes. 'Anyone else to rescue?' he asked impudently. To his surprise, Wallenberg replied, 'Yes, my office on Ulloi Road.'

On the way over, Wallenberg explained that he had learned that Arrow Cross thugs had taken over one of his offices. Once again Sandor Ardai witnessed Wallenberg's authority, functioning under almost divine protection. Inside, they found the office in complete disarray. Tough-looking young thugs lounged in chairs, staring defiantly at Wallenberg.

Raoul threatened that they would be reported to the new Minister of Foreign Affairs, Gabor Kemeny. 'Do you know I'm a foreign diplomat and that you are violating my rights? Do you know what this means?' he shouted in outrage. Then he brushed past one of the armed gunmen and moved to his desk, picking up papers from the floor.

Perplexed and curiously chastened, the hoodlums eventually withdrew and left the office.

One of his aides said later, 'We all wondered if there would be any reprisals, but to our surprise, nothing happened.'

Exactly 24 hours had passed. The death toll had risen to several hundred and posters appeared on billboards warning of reprisals against the Jews.

The Swedish Legation feared that Wallenberg's activities were endangering all their lives, but he remained unrepentant. As the Arrow Cross and the Nazis were mobilizing for a fresh onslaught against the Jews, the Wallenberg operation was also preparing to combat this with a new campaign of rescue missions.

He recruited Tom Veres to be his official photographer and to take photos secretly where necessary. A hidden camera was wrapped in Tom's shawl to capture some of the events. 'I want a complete documentary record of these horrors,' he told Tom. 'The world must know. We must never forget what is happening here.'

On the evening after the coup, Wallenberg was again issuing protective passes. Some were mere photocopies with his signature, given in the hope that they would offer some protection. On his instructions, everyone who had applied for a Swedish *Schutzpass* was to be given one and his staff delivered these personally to Jewish homes around the city. Although the curfew applied to every Jew in Budapest, *his* Jews were able to move throughout the city unhindered. From that day, Raoul carried a portable typewriter on the back seat of his Studebaker and a file containing blank passes.

Two days had passed since the coup when the large synagogues on Dohany Street and Rumbach Sebestayan Street were turned into *ad hoc* prisons. In a massive operation, 6,000 prominent Jews, including the Chief Rabbi Ferenc Heresi, were rounded up and held without food, water or toilet facilities. Armed guards blocked the entrances while inside the sanctuary, the group waited in nervous isolation.

One youth in the synagogue managed to slip through a toilet window at the rear of the building and telephoned 'Section C'. 'Can you get a message to Mr Wallenberg?' he said breathlessly. 'We're being held prisoner at the synagogue.'

When Raoul arrived at his office later that morning, he was handed a crumpled piece of paper with the scribbled message. He telephoned Charles Lutz, the Swiss chargé d'affaires, and hastily made arrangements to rescue as many as they could. Raoul called for Vilmos Langfelder to pick up Lutz and they drove to the synagogue.

The Studebaker pulled up outside the synagogue. From inside the elegant American car, Wallenberg and Lutz studied the fascist gunmen who loitered outside the building. They looked tough and ruthless. Taking a deep breath, Raoul opened the car door and, followed by Lutz, strode up the steps towards the front entrance. It was an impressive performance. Both men looked assured, in control. The gunmen at the gate stepped aside and allowed them in.

Raoul walked up to the main altar. 'Does anyone here hold a Swedish *Schutzpass*?' His voice boomed across the hall.

A murmur passed around the crowd. Several hands were raised high in the air. At the back of the hall the question was repeated.

'Yes, I do.'

'Me. I have a pass.'

'Here. I also.'

Raoul continued. 'All right. Everyone with a pass form an orderly queue by the entrance. *Orderly*.' He slammed his fist on the lectern to emphasize the point. 'It must be orderly.'

Stepping down from the altar, Raoul addressed the group of gunmen who had gathered below the podium, completely mystified by the unfolding events. Raoul explained in a matter-of-fact tone, 'These are Swedish citizens. You have no right to keep them here.' Speaking in perfect German, he continued, 'I order you to release them at once.'

He appeared pale but ferocious, and the combination proved intimidating for the Arrow Cross. They questioned him hesitatingly, but Raoul's sharp replies quelled their resistance. One eyewitness remarked that Wallenberg appeared like a magician who had cast a spell over his questioners. His handling of situations like this seemed uncanny, almost as if he was empowered by an unseen force.

At the main entrance to the synagogue the guards fingered the impressive *Schutzpasses*. Each was printed in two colours, featured the official stamp and seal of the Swedish Embassy and displayed the Royal emblem of Sweden. Each passport was personally signed by the Swedish Minister and Wallenberg. There was also a photograph to compare with each person who clutched a *Schutzpass* in their hands.

Beside the 'Swedes', a group of 'Swiss' Jews began to assemble.

Raoul crossed the hall, talking with one or two people as he passed. Somewhat intimidated by his authoritative and self-assured manner, the guards stepped aside and Raoul marched out of the synagogue at the head of his column of 'Swedes'. Lutz followed with his 'Swiss'. Some time later, combined protests freed the remainder of the hostages.

It had been a spectacular victory.

Chapter 9

❖❖❖

DEATH MARCH

Budapest, October 1944

On the same day that Eichmann returned to Budapest, he summoned the Jewish Council leaders to his headquarters at the Majestic Hotel. 'Yes, I'm back,' he declared, his face beaming with pleasure. 'My arm can still reach you.'

Eichmann outlined his strategy. As trains were being used for the war effort, the inventive SS leader had concocted a new idea. He would march the Jews to the border. Those left behind would be used as slave labour and held in concentration camps outside Budapest. A central ghetto would be constructed in the heart of Budapest. With the Russians advancing, Eichmann knew he would have to move fast.

Finally, the Nazi chief announced gloatingly, Szalasi's new government would not recognize any of the Swedish or foreign protective passes. That gambit was over.

The war against the Jews had been resumed. This time, the commander was drawing the net even closer. Taking aim, one last time.

The Jewish leaders gazed at each other in nervous apprehension. They heard his words but could not imagine what this meant. A march on foot? Who was to go? Surely not children? What about the old men? How would families manage? It can't be possible.

When Wallenberg heard the news, he refused to submit. 'We must fight for the right of the protective passes. We can't just surrender,' he argued incessantly. He telephoned several officials and tried to bargain for time. His manner could be deceptively unassuming. His network of contacts covered all levels of Hungarian society. In the past few weeks he had met a strikingly beautiful woman, Baroness Elizabeth Kemeny, the wife of the Arrow Cross Minister of Foreign Affairs. She had only recently married the Baron, apparently unaware that he was one of Hungary's most prominent fascists. Raoul had formed a liaison with her and the two became close friends. It was rumoured that she was half-Jewish and that Raoul had threatened to expose her secret, thus enlisting her co-operation.

Raoul arranged a secret meeting with the Baroness and warned that her husband would be hanged as a war criminal if he permitted this outrage to proceed. The 'International Jews' must be protected. It was up to her to influence her husband and stop this tragedy.

The Baroness responded with floods of tears and was comforted by Raoul. 'I am carrying his child,' she sobbed. 'I don't want my child to be born fatherless.' Raoul convinced her that she held a vital card in this game of life and death. This was the moment she must play it.

Under her influence, the Baron issued a statement broadcast over the radio. *The Swedish and foreign passports were to be recognized!*

Wallenberg had won another remarkable victory. Perhaps even he did not realize just how significant this was to prove in the days ahead.

Each new day brought reports of further atrocities. Almost every case involved a Jew. Somebody beaten up, somebody missing. The Arrow Cross had been in power for just over two weeks by then, but they were making up for lost time. And everywhere, Jews were reporting little miracles. Incredibly, Swedish *Schutzpasses* had saved many from a bullet in the head. At times, just the mention of Wallenberg's name seemed to be enough.

Raoul pushed himself tirelessly, working almost 20 hours every day, and expected the same from his staff. His offices had now moved from the Swedish Legation into the more dangerous area of Pest, amidst the Jewish district. In the offices a battery of secretaries hammered at typewriter keyboards, sending official complaints about Jewish outrages to every department in the Arrow Cross government. Other members of staff followed up hundreds of enquiries about Jews who had been arrested or who had disappeared. Wallenberg demanded an explanation in every case. He was representing the King of Sweden. If he did not get action, there would be trouble.

His own life was in constant danger. Warnings came through about a contract on his life. An Arrow Cross assassin was reported to be stalking him. An International Red Cross worker had overheard Eichmann cursing the Swedish diplomat and threatening, 'I'm going to kill that Jew-dog Wallenberg.' Later that month, an SS truck rammed Wallenberg's car at high speed, completely demolishing the front of the vehicle. At the time, Raoul was in another car.

Yet even Wallenberg could not halt the destruction. The countdown had begun. The moment Eichmann had been waiting for had arrived. All Jews, including women and children, were rounded up and ordered to march on foot to Hegyeshalom on the Austrian–Hungarian border, a journey of 125 miles. Destination: the death camps. The men were sent to a work camp in another location.

This was ultimate degradation, a nightmare come to life, with conditions so dreadful that even hardened Nazis complained. Jews were grabbed from shops and alleyways and forced to join the march. Some women wore light dresses and high heels; young children clutched the hands of elderly grandmothers and together trundled forward.

With no food, the group of marchers spent the night wherever the column halted. In the morning, bodies were found hanging from trees. Arrow Cross soldiers and Hungarian gendarmes herded them onwards. Stragglers and those who stumbled were executed on the spot – a bullet in the forehead or in the back of the head. Rifle butts crashed into the backs of young girls, smashing bones and ribs, as obscenities urged them forward.

Susan Tabor recalls, 'I felt totally alone, isolated. They had treated us like animals for so long that I came to believe that I was an animal. They had told us that we deserved to die so many times that I finally agreed with them.'

At the border at Hegyeshalom stood Eichmann and the SS men. The Jews had reached their final stop in Hungary. Numb with exhaustion, they obeyed Nazi orders and climbed on board the cattle trucks at the railway station.

'Where is this train going?' someone asked, subdued.

'Auschwitz,' came the reply.

Budapest, November 1944

The death march continued into November. Hard, driving rain and bitterly cold winds battered the aching bodies of young girls and elderly women, some clinging pathetically to young children. The route of the march was marked by the dead and the dying.

A brickyard in the northern suburb of Bekasmegyer transformed itself momentarily into an island of shelter in this ocean of suffering.

Late in the night, a group of women were herded into the enclosure by Arrow Cross guards. In the stampede, some girls stumbled, legs were broken. Without hesitation, gunmen stepped forward and they were shot dead. Once inside the brickyard, the women sank onto the cold earth, grateful for the temporary reprieve. But still they were not safe from the clutches of brutal guards and the young girls made easy prey.

The next morning, cold, hungry and dazed, they stumbled

outside and queued for the last part of their journey to the Austrian border.

From out of nowhere, a sleek American car drove up and pulled alongside the gate of the brickyard. A tall and elegant man in a fashionable hat and long leather coat stepped from the car. He carried a briefcase and a megaphone, which he raised to his mouth and began to speak. 'I will bring you food and water. Doctors and nurses will be with you shortly. Don't give up hope. I will return for anyone with a Swedish passport.' They stared at him as if in a dream. Then from the ranks, someone began a prayer. Quickly, other voices joined in. 'Hear, O Israel: The Lord our God, the Lord is one...'

To some he appeared like a phantom, mysterious and elusive. But then his name was whispered along the line. A glint of hope. When he did return, accompanied by Charles Lutz, the Swiss consul, and later with Per Anger, from the Swedish Embassy, the relief supplies were tragically inadequate.

Again, the versatile actor was summoned for another grand-stand performance. Wallenberg moved a wooden crate to the gate of the brickyard and bellowed once more into the megaphone. 'Anyone with a Swedish passport form an orderly line on this side,' he said, gesturing to his left. 'Those with Swiss passes on the other side. Portuguese passport holders in the middle...'

The Arrow Cross guards were taken by surprise. Baffled, they also began to submit to Wallenberg's instructions that this should be handled in an orderly fashion, insisting that the queues be maintained. It was a *tour de force*.

The women were in a daze. Disbelievingly, they shuffled towards the trucks that Wallenberg had organized and climbed aboard. 'Is this really happening?' one whispered. 'Thank God!' another exclaimed. 'Just thank God for this miracle.'

Without a moment to spare, Wallenberg had also bribed the local police chief to allow him to rescue some who did not have protective passes. 'I can save another 500 and take them back to

Budapest,' he said as he walked amongst the women. 'Forgive me, I cannot save everyone. I must save the young. I want to save a nation.' Then came the tragic moment of selection.

For a single instant he had the choice of life and death. He walked among them choosing girls and young women. Vilmos Langfelder followed beside him, filling in blank passes and listing their names in his register. It was a heartbreaking moment. All who remained behind would surely be gassed in Auschwitz.

Although Raoul Wallenberg had become well known in Budapest, his individual acts of courage were to confirm his legend among the Jews of Hungary.

Susan Tabor speaks for thousands when she states, 'Wallenberg made me feel human again. For the first time I had hope. In fact, I think that everyone felt different after his first visit. He showed us that we were not animals, that someone cared about us.'

At Eichmann's trial in 1961, Aryeh Breslauer testified that he had been sent to the border by Wallenberg with a typewriter and hundreds of *Schutzpasses*. Hundreds of Jews were rescued.

But it was never enough, and thousands still found themselves at Auschwitz. What restored some element of human dignity was that he, Raoul Wallenberg, and others inspired by his example, risked their lives to rescue everyone they could.

On the first day of the death march they rescued about 100 people who had been given protective passes. Each day they returned to snatch a few more. Everyone within reach received safe passage. Passports, travel cards, anything that looked official, sometimes literally scraps of paper, would be used to bluff the Arrow Cross guards and, like a conjurer, Wallenberg would dazzle his audience in order to escape with his precious bounty. Playing some hideous masquerade with the executioner, he refused to hand over 'his Jews'.

After placing those rescued from the brickyard in safe houses in Budapest, Raoul and Vilmos Langfelder drove back to the Austrian border where SS men were counting bodies before pushing them into cramped train carriages.

This time he carried a collapsible table, which he opened up right by the station gate beside armed Nazi guards. Langfelder brought the typewriter and laid out blank passes neatly in front of him as he sat on a fold-up chair. The register of 'Swedes' was also placed in front of him. The Wallenberg portable office was now ready for business. Ready to save Jewish lives.

Wallenberg appeared to be a man driven with a relentless urge, virtually an obsession. At luxurious cocktail parties in Stockholm he had discussed the fate of the Jews. Now he actually had the chance to do something to rescue them.

With Langfelder standing obediently by him and the SS men looking on quizzically, Raoul began his tirade. In front of him, the endless line of Jews waited as SS men counted out batches to be herded onto the cattle cars.

'I'm Wallenberg from the Swedish Embassy. You're holding my people. I demand their release.'

It was enough. The SS men had been trained to obey commands. Immediately they recognized a higher authority. Incredibly, no one questioned Raoul's orders.

His voice boomed across the yard as a chilly wind caused those in line to huddle together. 'Everyone with Swedish passports come out of that line and form an orderly queue on this side.'

With one foot in the executioner's cage, those people took a life-saving step to the side.

Raoul spotted a young girl in the line and approached her. 'Don't I know you? Didn't I give you a passport myself?'

The girl's eyes widened. Exhausted from the 100-mile march, she responded almost in slow motion. Like an actress remembering her lines, she fumbles in her pocket for a scrap of paper. It is an application for a driver's licence, crumpled and torn. She clutches it in her palm and offers it to him. Her eyes betray her panic.

Raoul smiles and takes the scrap of paper from her. It disappears into his pocket. Before the Nazi guards can follow the play,

Raoul grasps her slender arm and moves her out of the death queue. Now he shoves her to the side.

'Move, quickly. We haven't much time.' Talking fast, he realizes the charade cannot last long. The girl moves to the back of the queue of women saved by Wallenberg. Turning her head, she sneaks a glance at this extraordinary man. Moments later, the bedraggled group are led out by Vilmos Langfelder to Red Cross trucks parked at the side of the railway tracks. Silently the women climb on board, bound for Budapest...

Raoul used Joni Moser, a young, blond, blue-eyed Jew, as his assistant on several occasions because of his fluency in German and Hungarian. When news reached 'Section C' that 800 Jewish labour servicemen were being marched to Mauthausen concentration camp, Raoul and Joni raced to the frontier in the Studebaker, hoping to head them off. Again, the familiar tactic was activated. Raoul walked to the front of the group and asked those with Swedish protective passes to raise their hands. Behind the ranks, Moser was whispering to the men. He told John Bierman, 'On his order, I ran between the ranks and told the men to raise their hands, whether they had a passport or not. He then claimed custody of all who had raised their hands and such was his bearing that none of the Hungarian guards opposed him. The extraordinary thing was the absolutely convincing power of his behaviour.'

A few days after this incident, Moser was caught on the streets of Budapest by a Gestapo unit for questioning. He recalls, 'I thought it was the end for me.'

Standing in the street answering their questions, Moser's hopes began to fade until he spotted a friendly face. He continues the story: 'Just then Wallenberg happened to come by in his grand diplomatic car. He stopped and asked me to step forward for questioning. "Jump in, quick," he said – and before the astonished soldiers realized what had happened we were gone.'

Those were unforgettable times for Moser. 'Wallenberg was fantastic! His conduct, his power of organization, his speed in decision and action! What a strategist! Wallenberg was the initiator of the whole rescue action, remember that!'

Wallenberg was joined by several collaborators in the effort to save as many Jews as possible from the death march, but however valiant their efforts, it was still not enough to stop the whirlwind of Nazi force. By 2 November, about 20,000 Jews had marched the 125-mile, agonizing journey to the Austrian border. Auschwitz was on overload, with its crematoria operating night and day.

A further 13,000 Jews were 'in transit' and 10,000 had disappeared, many dying on the death march.

Still, the bloodhound was unsatisfied. Eichmann told his deputy, Dieter Wisliceny, 'The main thing is the statistics. Every Jew must be accounted for.'

Testimonies abound of Wallenberg's personal courage, charisma and, at times, sheer recklessness.

On one occasion Wallenberg saw a group of Jews about to be deported and asked them if they once held Swedish papers that had since been confiscated. Those alert enough raised their hands immediately and he made a list of names. An explosive argument with SS officers followed. As a result of his bravado, between 280 and 300 people escaped.

Wallenberg's appearances along the route of the death march were now legendary: snatching Jews from the roadside, he would return to his Budapest office to maintain a barrage of official protests to the Arrow Cross government. Under intense international pressure, the march was suspended. It was to little avail: deportations by train were resumed instead.

Once again, there were extraordinary scenes as Raoul made dramatic interventions at Budapest's central railway stations to rescue 'his Jews'.

Sandor Ardai, who had already witnessed one miracle when Vilmos was rescued, was given further glimpses of Raoul's courage and divine protection.

Sandor had driven Raoul to Jozsefvaros railway station where a trainload of Jews was about to leave for Auschwitz. Sandor told John Bierman: 'Raoul climbed up on the roof of the train and began handing in protective passes through the doors which were not yet sealed. He ignored orders from the Germans for him to get down, then Arrow Cross men began shooting and shouting at him to get away. He ignored them and calmly continued handing out passports to the hands that were reaching out for them. I believe the Arrow Cross men deliberately aimed over his head, as not one shot hit him, which would have been impossible otherwise. I think this is what they did because they were so impressed by his courage.

'After Wallenberg had handed over the last of the passports he ordered all those who had one to leave the train and walk to a caravan of cars parked nearby, all marked in Swedish colours. I don't remember exactly how many, but he saved dozens off that train, and the Germans and the Arrow Cross were so dumbfounded they let him get away with it.'

Dr George Basyai of Munich was in a batch of Jews at Ferencvarosi Palyaudvar freight station one night awaiting deportation. Elenore Lester reports, 'Suddenly a group of men came and said, "Those with Swedish passports should form a line..." My brother had such a passport, but I did not. My brother refused to move to that line without me. But then a very good friend, Laci Geiger, who was among the Swedish staff, detected me and my problem. He went to a man standing 50 yards away from us and spoke to him. This man, I found out later, was Raoul Wallenberg. He came to us, led me to the people inspecting passports and was standing next to me until the Nazi commander inspected our documents. Mr Wallenberg vouched for me so that I was able to join the group.'

The day after this rescue, Raoul returned to the Deli railway station in Buda to say farewell to Baroness Elizabeth Kemeny, now leaving Buda for exile and fearful about the future. She had been a useful ally and a trusted friend. Some had even whispered of a romantic liaison between the couple. Raoul entered her compartment with a bouquet of flowers for a private farewell. (Years later the Baroness tuned into a BBC world service news report to learn that her husband, along with all of Szalasi's Arrow Cross ministers, had been hanged as a war criminal.)

Raoul's door was always open and no one was turned away. Klari Balk called at his apartment at 4 a.m. She did not know him, nor did she possess a *Schutzpass*, but she was in great need. Her husband had been arrested and was about to be deported. 'Please, Mr Wallenberg, I beg of you to help me,' was a plea he could not refuse.

Mrs Balk told Elenore Lester, 'He dressed immediately and we drove to the station. Along the way he took all the details about my husband and filled out a Swedish passport for him. He went up to the Nyilas guards and showed them the passport. The guard went to the car where my husband was and called his name and he came out. The three of us left the station and returned to Wallenberg's flat. Then he settled us in a Swedish protected house at 1 Jokai Street.'

While the deportations by train continued, Raoul made commando-type raids on the railway station in order to grab Jews from the coaches and queues. He usually returned with astonished men and women who had experienced a miracle. But not every exercise was successful.

On one occasion, he was spotted by Captain Theodor Dannecker, notorious for his brutally effective deportation of French Jews that had earned him the nickname of 'the exterminating angel of the French countryside'. Dannecker and Wallenberg had tangled before and when the Swede was seen handing out *Schutzpasses* to a group of Jewish labourers about to be deported to Auschwitz, Dannecker stormed over, cursing the 'Jew dog'.

Raoul's customary diplomatic banter was not well received. Dannecker reached for his holster and drew out his pistol.

Instinctively, Raoul realized that the end of the line had been reached. He signalled to his photographer Tom Veres and the two hastily withdrew, with Dannecker virtually chasing them from the station, threatening revenge.

Chapter 10

❦

ON THE RUN

Budapest, December 1944

Just how long could the Germans hold out against the advancing Red Army? Raoul believed it was a desperate race against time. He had to cling on and offer Jews his protection. Every day mattered.

Eichmann was faced with the same question, but for him the issue concerned his own survival. Determined that a German defeat would not affect his central mission – the total annihilation of the Jews – he ordered all unprotected Jews, over 70,000 people, to move into a central ghetto. Six-foot-high planks were nailed down to frame the area and the hostages were moved in, leaving them dependent on the Arrow Cross for food and medicine.

The Jews living in Swedish safe houses had escaped this captivity, but the junta was now putting pressure on Raoul to arrange their emigration. His response was a tangled web of bureaucratic red tape. Raoul had already learned that Eichmann planned a bloody pogrom if he was forced to leave.

By 10 December, therefore, about 70,000 Jews were alone and unguarded, virtually sealed in the central ghetto. Meanwhile, about 30,000 Jews sheltered in the 'international ghetto', in Swedish safe houses run by Wallenberg. For the moment, the Swedish flag and Raoul's presence were sufficient to protect them, but no one could predict just how long that would last.

On 9 December the Russian army's offensive had reached the Danube at Vac, north of the city. The siege of Budapest had begun.

The day before, a courier had left for Sweden carrying Raoul's most recent report for the Foreign Office, informing them of current developments. His staff, numbering about 400 with their families, were living in 10 buildings that belonged to the Embassy and were thereby protected. They had been inoculated against epidemics such as typhoid and cholera. The report also confirmed that 'as far as can be ascertained, only 10 Jews with Swedish safe-conducts have up to now been shot in and around Budapest'. It was a staggering number given the circumstances.

The courier also carried Raoul's last letter to his mother:

Dearest Mother,

I don't know how to atone for my silence, and yet again today all you will receive from me are a few hurried lines via the diplomatic pouch.

The situation here is hectic, fraught with danger, and I am terribly snowed under with work ... Night and day we hear the thunder of the approaching Russian guns. Since Szalasi came to power diplomatic activity has been very lively. I myself am almost the sole representative of our embassy in all government departments. So far I have been approximately ten times to the Ministry of Foreign Affairs, have seen the deputy premier twice, the minister of the interior twice, the minister of supply once, and the minister of finance once.

I was on pretty close terms with the wife of the foreign minister. Regrettably she has now left for Meran [sic]. There is an acute lack of food supplies in Budapest, but we managed to stockpile a fair amount in advance. I have the feeling that after the [Russian] occupation it will be difficult to get home and I assume that I will reach Stockholm only around Easter. But all that lies in the future. So far, nobody knows what the occupation will be like. In any event, I shall try to get home as soon as possible.

I had firmly believed I would spend Christmas with you. Now I am compelled to send you my Christmas greetings and New Year wishes by this means. I hope that the longed for peace is not too distant.'

The letter was typed in German by a secretary who could not take dictation in Swedish. At the end Wallenberg scribbled, 'Love to Nina and her little one.'

Inspired by Wallenberg's example, a valiant group of neutral diplomats and relief workers formed an uneasy resistance to the fountainhead of evil. Throughout the previous six months, Wallenberg's adversary had been the notorious Adolf Eichmann and they clashed repeatedly in an epic struggle of good against evil. Raoul had first seen Eichmann across a smoky room in the Arizona nightclub, but the SS chief had dismissed him as just another weak, decadent aristocrat. Later he was to realize just how wrong this evaluation had been. Eichmann became infuriated with Wallenberg and ordered his assassination, but the plot failed.

Still, Eichmann was curious about this mystifying Swede and in mid-December he accepted an invitation to dinner with Wallenberg. Preoccupied with the day's activities, Raoul had forgotten about his 'guest' and enlisted the help of Lars Berg, his colleague at the Swedish Legation. Within a few hours, Berg had organized a sumptuous meal served on the finest china.

The dinner proved a success and afterwards the group retired to the living room, where coffee and liqueurs were served. On the horizon the distant thunder of the Russian guns lit up the Hungarian sky like firecrackers. Raoul turned out the lights in the living room and pulled back the curtains.

'The effect was tremendous,' Gote Carlsson told John Bierman. 'The horizon was bright red from the fire of thousands of guns as the Russians closed in on Budapest.'

' Letter reproduced courtesy of the Wallenberg family.

In his memoirs, Lars Berg describes what happened next:

Wallenberg, who on this occasion had no special wish to negotiate with Eichmann, started a discussion about Nazism and the
likely outcome of the war. Fearlessly and brilliantly he picked
Nazi doctrine apart, piece by piece, and foretold the total defeat
of its adherents. These were rather unusual words, perhaps, for a
Swede far from his country and more or less at the mercy of a
powerful German opponent. But that was always Wallenberg's
way. I think his intention was not so much to put his own views
forward as to pass on a warning to Eichmann that he would do
well to stop the deportation and extermination of the
Hungarian Jews.

Eichmann could scarcely conceal his amazement that anyone
should dare to attack him and criticize the *Führer*, but he soon
seemed to realize that he was getting the worst of the argument.
His propaganda phrases sounded hollow compared with Raoul's
intelligent reasoning. Finally, Eichmann said: 'I admit that you
are right, Herr Wallenberg. I have never believed in Nazism, as
such, but it has given me power and wealth. I know that this
pleasant life of mine will soon be over. My planes will no more
bring me women and wine from Paris, or delicacies from the
Orient. My horses, my dogs, my luxurious quarters here in
Budapest will soon be taken over by the Russians and I myself, as
an SS officer, will be shot on the spot.

'For me there will be no escape, but if I obey my orders from
Berlin and exercise my power harshly enough I may prolong my
respite for some time here in Budapest. I warn you, therefore,
Herr Legationssekretar, that I will do my best to stop you, and
your Swedish diplomatic passport will not help you if I find it
necessary to have you removed. Accidents do happen, even to a
neutral diplomat.'

With these words, Eichmann stood up to leave, but not at all
displaying any anger. With the imperturbable politeness of a well

educated German, he bade farewell to Raoul and thanked us for a particularly pleasant evening. Perhaps Raoul did not win very much by his direct attack, but it could sometimes be a great pleasure for a Swede to speak his mind to an SS officer.[2]

Budapest, 23 December 1944

Marshall Malinovsky's invading Red Army inched its way closer to Budapest with each passing skirmish. With only one road open, Szalasi and his top minister escaped, leaving Eichmann and the Nazis in a state of siege. But even in his final hours, Eichmann remained obsessed with the destruction of all Jews.

Eichmann had drawn up secret plans for his evacuation, leaving Nazi units to hold the city. The night before he was due to leave, 23 December, he turned up drunk at the Jewish Council's headquarters on Sip Street. He had planned to execute all its members in one fell swoop, but Wallenberg was one step ahead of him.

Through his network of informants, Wallenberg had learned of the execution plans and had warned the Council members to go underground. The guard on duty at the Council office was pistol-whipped and lay bleeding on the floor, while Eichmann ranted furiously. The guard did not reveal where the Council members were hiding, however, and Eichmann vowed to return.

With the Russian guns getting louder, Eichmann slipped through the net and left Budapest that day.

With Eichmann's escape the focus of evil was removed, but Hungary still remained within his influence. He had given the SS one final command to carry out before they evacuated: *Kill all the Jews in the central ghetto.*

The survival of the Jews depended on how quickly the Russians could reach the city, already encircled by Red Army troops. Wallenberg huddled by the wireless each night, listening intently

[2] Lars Berg, *What Happened in Budapest* (Stockholm, 1949).

to BBC broadcasts on troop movements and eagerly charting their progress, undoubtedly wondering just how long they could hold out.

On Christmas Eve, the day after Eichmann's escape, gunmen broke into a children's home run by the International Red Cross and shot toddlers as young as one and a half years. Other children were forced into the Danube and drowned. On Christmas Day, Nazis raided another children's home and shot many of the terrified youngsters.

The executions stunned Wallenberg and the other diplomats. It seemed there was nowhere further to fall. Also on Christmas day, Arrow Cross gunmen broke into a shelter at 25 Vilma Kiralyno Street, where two elderly women and three young children were shot. The rest of the children in the house were marched to nearby barracks. A lame 13-year-old boy who could not keep up was shot dead in the street. Another 14-year-old boy who had been shot in the leg and could not walk was executed in the home before the tragic march began.

Four days later patients, as well as doctors and nurses, from the Maros Street Hospital were tortured and killed.

The Christmas executions seemed to open the floodgates, unleashing an unprecedented new wave of terror. Jews were dragged out of buildings, stripped and robbed. Young Jewish girls were assaulted and raped, the words 'war whore' were tattooed on their arms, and they were mercilessly handed around the gangs that roamed the streets. Corpses piled up in the roads, some were hung from trees and lampposts, others were dumped in the Danube. Almost no one was safe.

In the final two months of the siege of Budapest, between 10,000 and 15,000 Jews were murdered.

Budapest, 1 January 1945

The wall of protection that Wallenberg had constructed for his Jews was crumbling. On New Year's Day, a Swedish house bearing the Swedish flag was attacked. Raoul raced to the scene just in time to save the occupants – about 80 Jews – from being murdered.

Not everyone could be saved. On 8 January 1945, 180 men, women and children were kidnapped from a protected house and assaulted in the street.

Early in January 1945, the last road out of Budapest was finally taken by the Red Army troops. Now the city was cut off from the rest of the world. Trapped inside were Nazi and Arrow Cross gunmen with their Jewish captives, and Raoul Wallenberg. With no authority other than the gun, everyone was at risk. The looting, rape and murder took on a new ruthlessness.

Father Andras Kun's notoriety increased with each passing day. In front of a trigger-happy gang, he declared open season on all Jews. He was responsible for a mass execution at a Jewish hospital in Buda, lining up patients and staff before a mass grave in front of an assassination squad. Brandishing his pistol, Father Kun ordered, 'In the holy name of Jesus Christ, fire!'

Mrs Vilmos Salter, another Arrow Cross killer, was among other women who derived pleasure from torturous amusements. Clutching a Thompson sub-machine-gun, she was known for burning the genitals of female victims or inserting a burning candle into the vaginas of screaming women.

Raoul went into hiding, emerging only after dark, keeping one eye on the shadows of the night. Father Kun handed out 'Wanted – Dead or Alive' posters of Raoul, calling for him to be shot on sight, and announced a reward for his capture.

The elusive Swede, however, had established a new set of contacts. In these final moments of the war, he had stumbled on an unlikely ally in Paul Szalai, a police official and member of the Arrow Cross, who had been revolted by the sadistic violence of party members. Through Szalai, Raoul learned of raids being planned and stayed one step ahead of the assassination squads.

Szalai also warned Raoul about assassins stalking him and placed two trusted policemen as his 24-hour bodyguard. From that time, Raoul went underground, never sleeping in the same apartment on consecutive nights. He changed licence plates on his car for every roadblock and also changed cars continually.

Despite the intense, compelling danger, Raoul refused to take shelter with the neutral diplomats, preferring to stay with 'his Jews'. Per Anger recalls his last meeting with Raoul in his memoirs:

> I urgently asked him to discontinue his activities and stay with us on the Buda side of the Danube. The Arrow Cross were obviously after him and he took great risks by continuing his rescue activities. However, Wallenberg refused to listen.
>
> While bombs were exploding all around us, we set out on a visit to SS headquarters, where, among other things, I was to request some kind of shelter for the embassy members. We had to stop the car repeatedly because the road was blocked with dead people, horses, burnt-out trucks, and debris from bombed houses. But danger did not stop Wallenberg. I asked him whether he was afraid. 'It is frightening at times,' he said, 'but I have no choice. I have taken upon myself this mission and I would never be able to return to Stockholm without knowing that I've done everything that stands in a man's power to rescue as many Jews as possible.' During the conversation with the SS general [Obergruppenführer Erich von dem Bach-Zelewsky], Wallenberg tried to obtain guarantees that the Jews in the Swedish houses would not be liquidated at the last minute. As usual, Wallenberg presented his errand skilfully and intelligently. The SS general listened sceptically but could hardly hide the fact that he was impressed by Wallenberg's behaviour. I particularly recall that part of the discussion when the German suddenly put the somewhat unexpected question to Wallenberg: *'Sie kennen Gyula*

Dessewffy sehr gut? Er hat sich übrigens in Ihrem Haus versteckt!' (You know G.D. very well? As a matter of fact, he is hiding in your house!) Dessewffy was a Hungarian aristocrat and journalist who had gone underground at the time of the German invasion. He was at that time active in the Hungarian resistance movement and the Germans were frantically looking for him.[1]

While on the run, hunted by Arrow Cross gunmen, Raoul turned up late one night at the house on Benczur Street to find his friend and photographer, Tom Veres. Tired, haggard and unshaven, the stubble on his chin gave him a rugged look.

Tom pulled him to one side and whispered, 'My parents have disappeared.' The words came slowly. Barely able to contain the tears, his eyes betrayed the fear in his heart.

Raoul touched Tom gently on the arm in an attempt to comfort him. 'I'm sorry, Tom,' Raoul replied, tightening his grip on the Hungarian's shoulders. 'It's too late.'

Tom's parents lived with a Swiss family in a building on Varoszmarty Square. An Arrow Cross squad hit the house unexpectedly and discovered a stash of food. The Swiss couple managed to escape, but Tom's parents were trapped. They were seen walking out of the house at gunpoint. Later, Tom was to learn that they had been shot dead and dumped in the Danube.

The danger proved only too real. Hoping to kidnap Wallenberg, armed gunmen attacked the Swedish Legation and ransacked the offices, taking the entire staff prisoner. When they realized that their captives did not include Raoul, the group were released, following negotiations.

Raoul continued the barrage of diplomatic missiles throughout the ordeal. His protests were phrased in diplomatic jargon and maintained the pretence of civilized communication between two governments. Meanwhile, he was bribing anyone

[1] Per Anger, *With Raoul Wallenberg in Budapest* (Stockholm, 1979).

who might have information about where the Arrow Cross were planning to strike next.

Within the sealed city, Wallenberg still managed to stay one step ahead of the assassination squads. Unlike traditional diplomats, he was ready to negotiate and make any kind of deal provided it saved lives. He had one final weapon: food!

When a horse died in the street, people rushed over to it with knives and hatchets, attacking it for the meat. Within moments, all that remained was the stripped carcass.

With tremendous foresight, Wallenberg had stockpiled secret warehouses of provisions and managed to feed the Jewish community from this hoard. Realizing that food was the strongest and virtually the only weapon he had to combat the unrelenting attacks against the Jews, he decided to negotiate with the enemy and entered their lair.

In the Town Hall's cellar, Wallenberg stepped cautiously. Was this a trap? All along the dimly lit corridor, armed guards leaned aimlessly against the wall. Inside the cellar's inner chambers, Sedey, chief of police, and Erno Vaina, the head of the Arrow Cross, faced Wallenberg. The meeting was tense, but Raoul showed no sign of nervousness. The Arrow Cross leaders knew that Wallenberg was their only chance of holding out against the Russian guns. With nowhere to turn, they accepted his terms.

'The attacks on the Jews must end. It's the only deal I can offer. If this stops, I will give you food,' Raoul declared.

Raoul followed this up with his customary written confirmation. Couched in diplomatic jargon, the note is flat and bizarre given the circumstances.

The deal did not halt all the attacks, but it had bought Raoul the one thing he needed most — *time!*

Budapest, January 1945

An even greater danger was lurking for the Jews in the central ghetto. Not forgetting Eichmann's orders for the total annihilation of the ghetto's population, 500 soldiers began to assemble near the Royal Hotel, waiting to be joined by 200 Arrow Cross gunmen. The target was the Jews in the central ghetto.

Eichmann's final command was now just minutes away from being carried out. Inside the ghetto, a sense of foreboding hung like a curtain. Their final hour would leave no mourners.

Behind the scenes, however, Wallenberg was engineering one ultimate, spectacular victory.

Szalai, Raoul's informant inside the Arrow Cross, sent him an urgent message through a Christian go-between, Karoly Szabo, who was safe on the streets.

Finding Wallenberg in his secret hideout, Szabo spoke breathlessly. 'They're going to kill all the Jews in the central ghetto. Within the hour they will all be dead. I think it's too late.'

Wallenberg received the news with little emotion. Physically he was exhausted, his eyes bloodshot – he had slept barely a few hours in the past few nights. Nonetheless, during his six months in Hungary he had learned one vital lesson: it's never too late.

'No,' he said solemnly. 'We mustn't give up hope. It's one minute to midnight.'

Raoul sat at his desk and took some letterhead with the Royal seal from one of the drawers. 'There's only one man who can stop this now,' he said, addressing himself as well as Szabo. 'Give him this message, but hurry.' He scribbled something on the diplomatic paper.

SS General August Schmidthuber was weary. He too was more concerned about his immediate future than his loyalty to the Reich. That monument was now crumbling and Schmidthuber was knee-deep in its ashes.

It was too dangerous for Raoul to be seen on the streets, so he could not visit the Nazi General personally. He walked Szabo to the entrance of the apartment where he had taken shelter and instructed the go-between to take his message personally to Schmidthuber. He said, 'Tell Schmidthuber that if this pogrom proceeds and the Jews die, I will personally testify at the War Crimes Tribunal and see that he is hanged for murder.'

With extraordinary perception, Wallenberg had pinpointed the Nazi General's weakness. When Schmidthuber received the message, his heart sank. He paced the floor of his office at the Majestic Hotel as he recalled the Swedish diplomat's accomplishments over the last six months.

Wallenberg's written threat had reached Schmidthuber at the crossroads. Would it be Eichmann's legacy that prevailed, or Wallenberg's resistance? Thousands of Jewish lives hung in the balance as the Nazi and fascist gunmen continued to assemble in front of the central ghetto.

Finally, Schmidthuber ended the suspense by picking up his telephone and cancelling the slaughter.

Two days later, when the Russian troops arrived, they discovered over 70,000 Jewish survivors. Everyone in the ghetto had survived through the influence of one man.

Chapter 11

♦♦♦

FINAL DAYS IN BUDAPEST

Budapest, 8 January 1945

Wallenberg had remained with 'his people' inside the sealed city during the siege of Budapest. He went underground to dodge Arrow Cross gunmen and his whereabouts were held in great secrecy. He took refuge first at the Hezai Bank, where the vault had become a shelter for several Jewish families as well as Vilmos Langfelder and Tom Veres.

Szalai, Raoul's Arrow Cross contact, visited him and was taken on a tour of the refuge. 'Did you ever see a bank vault anywhere in the world which held greater treasure than this one?' Wallenberg asked the Arrow Cross man. 'Human lives are much greater than silver or gold.'

Raoul told Szalai that he wanted to contact the Russians to get food for the Jews in the ghettos. Supplies were running out and starvation was inevitable. The food crisis in late December had prompted both Raoul and the Swiss diplomat, Harold Feller, to make contact with the Russians, but Feller had been abducted by the Arrow Cross and had disappeared.

On 11 January, three days after he had taken shelter at the Hezai Bank, Raoul decided it was too risky to stay. 'I must keep moving,' he told the group who remained behind.

At midnight, Raoul slipped stealthily out of the Bank and disappeared into the January darkness. In an unmarked car, he headed for the villa on Benczur Street, the headquarters of the Red Cross, where he was welcomed by George Wilhelm. For the next three nights, Raoul began to unwind. He slept late and ate well, with food prepared by the chef of the Astoria Hotel.

With time on his hands, he looked over notes he had been making during the last few weeks. One file contained an outline for a rehabilitation programme for a postwar relief organization.

With a team of Jewish advisers, he had been working secretly on the project in one of the protected houses. Raoul had prepared a report with suggestions for restoring the economic life of the city (including the return of properties and businesses to Jewish proprietors) and an emergency action team to deal with the starvation and disease that were threatening. The plan for an autonomous agency encouraged the value of self-help, emphasizing, 'We want to use the rapid routes which are offered by private action and private supervision. We will accept government and national assistance and incorporate it in our activity providing it will not cause delay in providing the assistance.'

Raoul also commented in the report that his own staff were selected for three qualities – 'compassion, honesty and initiative'.

He had already drafted a fundraising appeal to launch the project. The introductory text stated:

I ask your indulgence if I use the first person to address you. I promise that this will be the first and last time and I am only doing it because I am well known as the head of the Humanitarian Section of the Royal Swedish Legation. Thousands of you have helped organize my rescue operations and now I am appealing for your continued assistance for relief work. As you know, I am a citizen of a neutral country, but I think it is fair to say that neither I nor my country have ever looked on neutrality as a comfortable, easy way to avoid suffering. On the contrary, my countrymen have often proven themselves even more sensitive to human suffering than those who suffer. For many months now I have witnessed the suffering of the Hungarian people and, if it is not too presumptuous to say so, I think I have participated in it spiritually to such an extent that it has now become my suffering. Because of my involvement, I have been able to recognize the great need for speedy humanitarian relief and reconstruction activities.[1]

He is also thought to have made a detailed list of assets held by Jewish families. In the wrong hands, this information could be explosive. He had probably heard reports of foreign banks holding accounts of Holocaust victims, an event that continues to haunt those implicated in this secretive episode. The full extent of the theft of money, gold, jewels, art and property is still unfolding today.

After several days at the Red Cross hideout, Raoul ventured out. His first stop was the office on Ulloi Street, where even more applications for Swedish protective passes waited for his signature. He signed them but thought it unnecessary. 'It's almost over,' he told one colleague. 'We're a part of history now.'

Langfelder drove Wallenberg to the Town Hall, where Szalai had taken refuge. Together they discussed the future. Wallenberg told Szalai that he wanted to make a radio broadcast to launch his relief programme and added, 'But first I have to clear things with Malinovsky and the Red Army.'

Wallenberg continued, 'As soon as the city is liberated, I want you to meet Malinovsky. Then I'm taking you to Sweden, my friend, to meet the King of Sweden. I want the world to know what you have done and how you have helped our mission. You'll not be forgotten, you'll see.'

Szalai had provided Wallenberg with vital information when it was most necessary. With his co-operation, Raoul was able continually to outsmart the Arrow Cross gunmen. He had also provided

[1] Fredrik von Dardel, *Wallenberg-fakta kring ett ode* (Stockholm, Proprius Forlag, 1970).

personal protection for Raoul himself and kept him safe during the last few weeks of the siege.

From the Town Hall, Langfelder headed the Studebaker towards the Swiss Legation's office, where Raoul collected assorted documents and over 200,000 pengös that had been hidden for relief supplies.

That night the Russian troops' gunfire could be heard just streets away from No. 16 Benczur Street where they had taken refuge. Members of a German suicide squad were fighting it out in the Royal Palace; snipers on rooftops and gunmen in doorways were the last column of opposition.

Wallenberg, Langfelder and the others in the Benczur Street house sat huddled together in the basement kitchen with gunfire ringing in their ears. No one slept that night. Early the next morning, a street patrol working house by house stepped through the debris. The Russian liberators were there.

The Russians blamed the Hungarian civilians for sympathizing with the Nazis, thus prolonging the siege. It has been suggested that the Russian soldiers were granted an unconditional three-day pillage of Budapest as a reward, the spoils of war. Whatever the truth, the Red Army's appetite covered everything from gold watches to women.

Budapest itself was in ruins. The city had no electricity or water, and little food. All the bridges across the Danube had been blown up by the retreating Nazi soldiers. Across the river in Buda, only four buildings were still standing. About 800 other buildings were reduced to smoking rubble.

A midnight-hour execution squad tried to hit as many Jews as possible in the central ghetto. About 3,000 were killed and 246 bodies were found decomposing.

Nevertheless, about 120,000 Hungarian Jews had survived. About 70,000 men, women and children had been found alive in the central ghetto. Another 25,000 or so had survived in the inter-national ghetto, and about 25,000 were found hiding in Christian homes, monasteries, convents, church basements and other sanctuaries. At least 100,000 people owed their lives directly to Raoul Wallenberg.

Raoul Wallenberg encountered his Russian liberators on the morning of 13 January, when the street patrol stumbled on the group huddled in the Benczur Street house. On the field telephone, the patrol's chief officer summoned Major Dimitri Demchinkov, who arrived in Benczur Street within half an hour.

Raoul introduced himself and presented his credentials as a Swedish diplomat. He also explained his role in the last few months, watching the Major's face as he frowned with puzzlement.

Raoul and Langfelder, accompanied by Demchinkov, spent that night at the Russian headquarters on Queen Elizabeth Street. The commander of the Zuglo District, General Tchernishev, listened, somewhat mystified, as details of this curious mission were explained. Raoul insisted that he must reach the Red Army commander, Marshall Malinovsky, and the provisional government, who had set up their headquarters in the eastern city of Debrecen, 120 miles away from central Budapest.

Tchernishev granted permission and issued the regulatory permit. He also provided Raoul with a two-man armed escort, headed by Demchinkov.

The morning of 17 January 1945 was the last day Raoul Wallenberg and Vilmos Langfelder were seen as free men.

They returned in the Studebaker to the house on Benczur Street. Raoul collected his rucksack and his funds, about 222,000 pengős, a vast amount of money in those days. From Benczur Street, Langfelder drove Raoul to the Tatra Street shelter where some money was handed over for running expenses for the relief operation and for feeding his staff, as well as those in the Swedish protected houses.

'I'll be back from Debrecen in about a week,' Raoul told them. He appeared relaxed. Glancing out of the window at his Russian escort, he commented, 'I don't know if I'm their guest or their prisoner.'

Laszlo Peto, one of Raoul's close friends, planned to accompany him for part of the journey. The Studebaker stopped outside the Swedish hospital started by Raoul, and he and Laszlo entered the building for last-minute consultations about funds. When they stepped back into the street, Raoul slipped on the ice. The hospital manager, Paul Nevi, reached over to help him up. As Raoul dusted the snow from his leather coat, two elderly men with yellow stars walked past them, taking their first few footsteps in freedom. Raoul noticed them and, turning to Paul, said, 'I'm pleased to see that my mission has not been in vain.'

After leaving the Tatra Street house, the Studebaker collided with a Russian army truck. Laszlo notes, 'The Russians were furious and dragged Langfelder out of the driver's seat. God knows what might have happened, but just at that moment the motorcycle with the Russian major arrived and he put an end to the altercation.'

Laszlo changed his mind and decided to wait in Budapest for news of his family, who had gone underground during the siege and were still missing. The Studebaker stopped on the corner of Benczur Street, Laszlo stepped out, shook hands with Raoul and turned to walk down the street back to the office. After taking a few steps, he turned and waved once again to Raoul, inside the moving vehicle. Laszlo watched the Studebaker head off towards the east.

No one would ever see Raoul Wallenberg again in freedom.

Raoul Wallenberg had packed a lifetime's experience into his six months in Hungary. The last few days had been taken at breakneck speed. Like a modern-day Daniel, he had reached into the lion's den to rescue the lost.

For a time, it had seemed as though he was untouchable, protected by some unseen guardian angel. But now he was skating on thin ice.

Although he did not realize it, time had run out for Raoul Wallenberg.

Part Two

MYSTERY

Chapter 12

✦✦✦

WHERE WAS RAOUL?

Cell 123, Lubyanka Prison, Moscow

What happened to Raoul Wallenberg has remained an unsolved mystery.

On 16 January, the Soviet Foreign Ministry informed the Swedish Ambassador in Moscow, Staffan Soderblom, that Wallenberg was in Russian hands, taken into custody for his own protection. At the time, the Swedes were more concerned about the other diplomats in Hungary, as contact had been cut off at Christmas and the entire Swedish Legation, including Minister Danielsson, Per Anger and Lars Berg, had all gone into hiding.

In Stockholm, Raoul's mother Maj and his stepfather Fredrik von Dardel, a nuclear physicist, became anxious. In February his mother called on the Soviet Ambassador to Sweden, Madame Alexandra Kollontai, who informed Maj that her son was safe. Shortly afterwards, Madame Kollontai repeated the message to Ingrid Gunther, the wife of the Swedish Foreign Minister. This time, the Soviet Ambassador added a note: it would be better 'not to make a fuss' about the matter. In good time, Raoul would return.

On 8 March 1945, the Russian-controlled Kossuth Radio broadcast the news that Wallenberg had been murdered *en route* to Debrecen by 'agents of the Gestapo'. The Swedish Foreign Office immediately cabled Soderblom in Moscow to seek clarification from the Russians.

On 17 April, the Swedish Legation from Hungary, led by Minister Danielsson, returned home to Stockholm via Moscow and Leningrad. Standing on the Stadgard quay, Raoul's mother Maj turned away in tears when she realized her son was not with Per Anger and the others who had returned.

Where was Raoul Wallenberg?

Budapest, 17 January 1945

Sometime during 17 January, just outside Budapest, Raoul Wallenberg was handed over to agents of SMERSH, an acronym for Russian counterintelligence during World War II. It meant literally 'Death to Spies', and was a division within the NKVD, soon to become the KGB, that dealt with all spies and agents.

SMERSH agents now had charge of this mysterious character who claimed to be Swedish and on a mission funded by the United States. His cover: rescuing Jews. The Studebaker and the money and valuables that Wallenberg was carrying were confiscated.

The NKVD took Raoul and Vilmos Langfelder by train to Moscow via Romania. They stopped *en route* at a town called Jassy and dined at a restaurant called Luther. In Moscow, the NKVD reminded both the diplomat and his driver that they were in protective custody and not under arrest, confirming what Ambassador Kollontai had told Raoul's mother in Stockholm.

A short sightseeing trip was arranged in Moscow which included a run on the legendary Moscow subway. The last station on the whistle-stop tour was Derzhinskaya Square. On one side of the square was a four-storeyed building that housed the former offices of the Rossiya Insurance Company. Next door was a modern building. Curiously, the top floor had no windows.

Together Raoul Wallenberg and Vilmos Langfelder, accompanied by their protectors, climbed the stairs and entered the notorious Lubyanka Prison, the headquarters of the KGB. Vilmos followed Raoul into the ominous hall by the entrance and then into an anteroom.

Lubyanka Prison is the central clearing house for all prisoners inside Russia. A black joke amongst 'guests' has it that the Lubyanka is the tallest building in Russia. From the top floor you can see Siberia.

As newcomers, both men were processed – fingerprints, photographs, and the legendary brown manila file with their name, number and case description stamped in the top right-hand corner. The file never leaves Lubyanka Prison and charts the prisoner's itinerary through the Gulag prison system. Raoul's prison registration card was dated 6 February 1945.

Once inside Lubyanka, Raoul Wallenberg and Vilmos Langfelder were separated. They were never to see each other again.

Raoul followed his guard down a dimly lit corridor with a black stripe all along the wall. They stopped at cell 123 and Raoul was ushered inside. His cellmates were Gustav Richter, a former Nazi officer under Eichmann in Bucharest, and Otto Scheur, who had served the Third Reich on the Eastern Front.

Outside prison walls, Wallenberg had fought tirelessly against men like these, but in cell 123 the three became acquaintances, faced now with a common enemy.

The cell door had a tiny window flap for the guards to peer through, and a small window high up on the opposite wall provided the only ventilation in the squalid, claustrophobic room. The roughly-made wooden cots were supplemented by a table and a box, used as a toilet. Drab dark green, almost black, walls completed the decor. Talking at night was forbidden. Each day, guards took them to the roof of the building for exercise. The 18-foot wall prevented them from peering over to the street below, but the noise of traffic could still be heard. The honking of car horns, the squealing of tyres and slamming of brakes, the car engines ticking over ... these sounds became their sole contact with the world outside.

The first night Raoul assumed would be his last in cell 123. Tomorrow, the misunderstanding would be cleared up and forgotten.

Richter said Raoul told him that the journey by train from Hungary to Moscow had taken five days. He recalled Raoul's concern about his mother and relatives. 'What will my family say when they learn that I am in prison?' The question was one of nervous anxiety. Aware that a criminal record would not increase his future prospects back home in Stockholm within the elite Wallenberg dynasty, he expressed a natural concern.

About the beginning or middle of February, after a few days in cell 123, Raoul drafted a written appeal to the Lubyanka Prison director, protesting at his detention and requesting permission to contact the Swedish Embassy in Moscow.

Raoul remained in good spirits, convinced that he would be released when he was identified. Ironically, however, it was his identity that sealed his fate.

Raoul's first interrogation by the NKVD (KGB) during his sojourn in cell 123 was undertaken by a plainclothes officer. When Raoul entered the interrogation room, the officer said, 'Ah, yes, it's you. We know all about you. We know who you are. You belong to a big capitalist family in Sweden.'

The interrogation lasted about an hour to an hour and a half. When Raoul returned to cell 123, he looked puzzled. He told Richter and Scheur, 'They think I'm a spy. I've been accused of spying for America and possibly for Britain as well.'

That same month, the Yalta Conference was to settle the shape of postwar Europe. Hitler and Himmler had both committed suicide and Adolf Eichmann was using the Odessa trail to cover his tracks. He would spend the next 16 years in freedom and even father a son.

In March 1945, Richter was moved to cell 91 on the sixth floor of Lubyanka Prison. Before he left, Raoul slipped him a piece of paper with his name and the address of the Swedish Foreign Office on it. But Richter was searched before entering his new cell and the paper was confiscated.

Raoul was also moved shortly after this to join Wilhelm Roedel, formerly a counsellor at the German Embassy in Bucharest, and Hans Loyda, a Czech-born interpreter.

After Raoul had settled his prison belongings onto his cot, he introduced himself to his new cellmates. Roedel and Loyda both smiled in recognition when they learned his name. They had heard of him and his mission in Hungary through their previous cell-mate – Vilmos Langfelder. When Raoul was told that his driver was sharing a cell close to them, he asked for his cigarette ration to be passed on to Vilmos.

Sometime in April 1945, the door to his cell was unlocked and he was ordered to leave. Perhaps he walked down the dingy passage of Lubyanka Prison with his hopes rising. Bundled into an unmarked police van, he may have wondered where this midnight journey would lead.

Lubyanka Prison was just the first stage of prison life. It was here that individuals were catalogued, registered and then cata-pulted forward into the Gulag system.

The police van crossed Moscow that night and, after a short journey, entered Lefortovo Prison, a massive fortress shaped like the letter K. Lubyanka had marked his card. Lefortovo was to engulf him.

Did he question his guards? Was he clubbed into silence? Did he have time to notice the wire netting across the staircase at each landing to prevent prisoners from committing suicide by jumping from the higher floors?

He was led onto the third floor. The dark metal door of cell 151 opened and he was ushered in. What were his thoughts when the prison door shut behind him?

Cell 151, Lefortovo Prison, 1945

Cell 151 in Lefortovo Prison was fairly spacious, the room being 10 feet long by eight feet wide with three beds, a table, and a basin with running water. The window high above on the far wall had a metal covering. Similar to the Lubyanka, the door had a peephole flap, which the guards used regularly.

Claudio de Mohr was asleep in cell 152 when he heard two new prisoners being moved into cell 151. Mohr was the former Italian consul in Bulgaria, and he had been captured by Russian troops at the Bulgarian–Turkish border. He recalls:

> At first we did not contact them. Very early one morning I heard our neighbours in Cell 151 communicating a long time by knock-ings with another cell. We grasped later half of the report, and we could understand that one of the prisoners in German related that he had been arrested by the Russians in Budapest in January 1945. Then we tried to get direct connection with the prisoners in 151 and in this way we learnt that one of our neighbours was the German councillor of legation Willy Roedel and the other Mr R.W. from the Swedish Legation in Budapest. We were so surprised that a Swedish diplomat had been arrested that we many times asked for confirmation, which was given to us.[']

Raoul easily cracked the prison communications code, telegraphing his messages with the other prisoners on the water pipe in the corner of his cell – one tap for 'A', two taps for 'B', and so on. He tapped regularly and thus other inmates heard his extraordinary story.

Raoul and Roedel were later moved to cell 203 on the Lefortovo Prison's fourth floor, directly above cell 151, their original cell on arriving at the prison.

Cell 203 was in the 'diplomatic wing' of the prison, where several foreigners were being held. During their imprisonment in cell 203, they exchanged messages with several prisoners.

Karl Supprian, from the German Embassy in Bucharest, shared a cell with the Italian Claudio de Mohr. He recalled, 'I was very

---

' Swedish Foreign Office White Books on Raoul Wallenberg.

surprised to hear that a Swedish diplomat was in prison and asked Roedel to confirm this so that there should be no mistake. Roedel repeated the message, yes, he had shared a cell with Wallenberg, a Swedish diplomat who had been arrested in Budapest in 1945.'[2]

Heinz Helmut von Hinckeldey, a German major, stated, 'I communicated with Wallenberg in German. Wallenberg gave the name of his family's bank in Stockholm as his address. He told me he had refused to make any statement to his interrogators citing his diplomatic status.' Wallenberg told Hinckeldey that he had repeatedly asked to contact the Swedish Embassy in Moscow, to no avail.[3]

One floor below Wallenberg and Roedel were Ernst Wallenstein and Bernhard Rensinghoff, who shared cell 105, both of whom communicated regularly with cell 203 through the prison telegraph system.[4]

Next door to cell 203, Willi Bergemann was imprisoned in cell 202. Bergemann said, 'Wallenberg was a keen knocker. He knocked in perfect German. If he wanted to speak to us he would knock five times in succession before commencing.'[5]

Wallenberg was separated from his Hungarian friend and driver, Vilmos Langfelder, on their arrival in Lubyanka Prison in February 1945, and the two never met again. Held as an accomplice, Langfelder was also considered a spy.

Langfelder's first cellmates in Lubyanka were the German Roedel and the Czech Hans Loyda, both POWs. He was interrogated on two occasions about events in Budapest leading to their arrest. On 18 March, Langfelder was moved to Lefortovo Prison and held incommunicado for three days. He was then taken to cell 105 and joined Erhard Hille, a German corporal. Langfelder told Hille that Wallenberg had tried to contact the Russian

[2] Ibid.
[3] Ibid.
[4] Ibid.
[5] Ibid.

headquarters in Hungary 'to try to prevent further bombardment at the [Swedish] Legation block, as there were no bullet-proof shelters there'. Hille was Langfelder's prison cellmate from 22 March to 6 April, when the German was moved to cell 287 in Moscow's Butyrki Prison. He never saw Langfelder again, but met several foreign POWs who had shared cells with Langfelder, including Hans Loyda.

Loyda told Hille that when Langfelder was moved from his cell, on 18 March, he was replaced by Raoul Wallenberg. Further details about Wallenberg's interrogation emerged. Wallenberg had been questioned several times by the NKVD. 'The leaders of the inter-rogation said that Raoul Wallenberg was a rich capitalist,' Loyda reported.

During 1945, Langfelder's cellmates in Lefortovo Prison included Horst Kitschmann, Ernst Huber and a Finn named Pelkonen. In conversation with his cellmates, the details of the arrest of Langfelder and Wallenberg in Budapest were revealed.

One fact emerged clearly: Wallenberg and Langfelder had been arrested by the NKVD's SMERSH section. *Wallenberg and Langfelder were held to be spies!*

Chapter 13

❦

DIPLOMATIC DISASTERS

Moscow – Stockholm – New York, April 1945

During 1945, Raoul Wallenberg seemed in good spirits despite his imprisonment, first in Lubyanka and then Lefortovo Prison. His first few months of imprisonment were to prove disastrous on the diplomatic front, however.

The Swedish Ambassador in Moscow, Staffan Soderblom, was to play a pivotal role in the Wallenberg mystery. He was the architect of two catastrophes.

The first occurred on 10 April 1945, when Averell Harriman, the American Ambassador in Moscow, offered assistance in determining Raoul's whereabouts. Without consulting Sweden, Soderblom snubbed the US Ambassador's offer of help. It would take 20 years for this serious error to be made public.

Seven days after Harriman's offer, the Swedish Legation's Hungarian staff who had been Raoul's colleagues in Budapest returned to Stockholm.

On 14 April Soderblom cabled the Foreign Office in Stockholm stating that Wallenberg had 'probably been killed' and he had no hope of the matter being 'cleared up'. The Swedish Ambassador in Moscow held the same view as the Soviet government.

Prompted by Sweden, Soderblom peppered the Soviet authorities with official requests into Wallenberg's location, but pursued the case with little zeal.

Back home in Sweden, a front-page article in Stockholm's leading newspaper, *Dagens Nyheter*, featured Raoul's extraordinary secret mission in Hungary and interviewed a Hungarian Jew who had arrived in Sweden. That same month, the *New York Times* of 26 April 1945 published an article about the disappearance of Raoul Wallenberg.

Lefortovo Prison, 1945–6

Raoul may have been hopeful of an early release as he paced his cell floor in Lefortovo Prison in 1945, but the days turned to weeks and the weeks to months, with Christmas approaching. Just one year ago he had written home to his mother speculating about his homecoming. He was equally concerned about his future job prospects.

In the summer of 1946, Raoul composed an appeal to Josef Stalin. First, he discussed the contents of the letter with his cell-mates through the prison telegraph, tapping messages on the water pipe in the corner of his cell.

Wallenberg talked to Rensinghoff, Wallenstein and von Rantzaw. Together, they agreed that the text should be in French.

The appeal spelled out the same question: I am a diplomat – why should I be held in prison? Can I please contact the Swedish Embassy in Moscow or the Red Cross, either in writing or preferably in person?

There was no direct reply to the appeal, but Wallenberg was summoned for another interrogation.

When Wallenberg returned to his cell, he telegraphed a message to Rensinghoff. 'The NKVD said that mine was a political case,' Raoul tapped on the water pipe. And with typical secret police logic they had charged, 'If you are innocent, then you should prove it.'

Wallenberg told Rensinghoff more of what his interrogators had said. 'The best proof that Wallenberg was guilty was the fact that the Swedish Legation in Moscow and the Swedish government had done nothing about his case.'

'Nobody cares about you,' the NKVD officer had said bluntly. 'If the Swedish government or its Embassy had any interest in you, they would have been in contact long ago.'

Rensinghoff could not see Raoul's face as he tapped out this lonely, pitiful message, and the knockings through the wall did not betray Raoul's feelings.

Raoul was interrogated on one further occasion during 1946 and again communicated with Rensinghoff. When asked if he would be given a trial and officially charged, the NKVD interrogator had told Raoul, 'For political reasons, you will never be sentenced.'

Moscow – Stockholm, 1946

If Raoul Wallenberg believed the world was concerned about him, he would have been devastated to have learned about events outside his prison walls.

Eduard af Sandeberg, a Swedish foreign correspondent in Berlin, had been released from a Soviet prison after his arrest as a spy, and returned to Sweden in June 1946. During his debriefing at the Foreign Office, he said he had been imprisoned with a Romanian and a German, both of whom had encountered a Swedish diplomat named Wallenberg.

Sandeberg knew nothing of the case and was unaware of the electrifying nature of this information. The Foreign Office made no attempt to follow it up.

It would take almost 10 years for Sandeberg's 'German' to appear in the West. Erhard Hille was released in 1955 and spoke of his personal encounter with Raoul Wallenberg. Other POWs would also relate accounts of this mysterious Swedish prisoner buried alive in a Soviet prison.

The second catastrophe occurred in Moscow at around the same time as Sandeberg's debriefing in Stockholm. Once again, the chief architect of the disaster was the Swedish Ambassador in Moscow, Staffan Soderblom.

By June 1946, Raoul Wallenberg had spent 16 months in captivity. Not far from his prison cell in Lefortovo Prison, a meeting took place that would virtually seal his fate for the next decade.

Soderblom was granted a personal audience with Josef Stalin and the Swedish Ambassador was distinctly flattered and impressed. During their conversation, Soderblom mentioned the disappearance of Raoul Wallenberg and the Russian dictator promised to look into the matter. Soderblom spelled out the name and Stalin reached across the desk and wrote the name down on a pad in front of him.

Wallenberg.

Unprompted, Soderblom then continued, 'I personally think Wallenberg was killed in Budapest.' He went on to suggest that the Russian dictator should issue an official statement confirming that investigations had provided no further clue or information about the missing diplomat. 'This would be in your own interest,' Soderblom explained, 'as there are people who would draw the wrong conclusions if there was no explanation.'

Stalin replied, 'I promise you that the matter will be investigated and cleared up. I shall see to it personally.'

This astonishing exchange was to be covered up by Swedish Foreign Office confidentiality. For 34 years it was an official secret, only released in 1980 when 1,900 pages of secret documents on this extraordinary case became public.

Perhaps no other single incident was to play such a crucial role in Raoul's fate. Three months after Soderblom's meeting with Stalin, the Swedish government was told not to enquire further. The Wallenberg case was closed.

That same year, the Swedish public learned the details of Raoul's daring exploits in Hungary through the publication of a book. *Fighter for Freedom* by Rudolf Philipp also contained a cohesive and convincing argument that Raoul was still alive and in captivity. Philipp and Raoul's parents, Maj and Fredrik von Dardel, hoped the book would arouse interest and sympathy in Raoul's case. A committee was formed in Stockholm to keep the story alive.

In Stockholm's Foreign Office, Raoul Wallenberg was clearly an embarrassment, an irritation they thought would just fade away in time. In Hungary, however, he was a legend and in August 1946 the Jews of Budapest arranged for Phoenix Street, in the heart of the wartime ghetto, to be renamed Wallenberg Street.

Chapter 14

▼▼▼

THE RUSSIANS REPLY

Lefortovo Prison, 27 July 1947

The third year of Raoul's imprisonment – 1947 – was to prove devastating. It was the year the Russians took action. Only Wallenberg's KGB file will reveal exactly who Stalin designated to deal with the case of the missing diplomat.

On the night of 27 July, the prison telegraph was buzzing. In Lefortovo, the rattling of keys and the sounds of doors being opened and closed were closely followed by the shuffle of feet as prisoners were marched to the interrogation cells. The focus of the long night's investigation was Raoul Wallenberg.

The interrogations began at about 10 p.m. and continued all through the night. No one was exactly sure what they wanted. An NKVD Colonel conducted the interviews with a Lieutenant-Colonel acting as interpreter.

Richter was first.

He was woken from sleep, and marched down to the interrogation cell to face the two solemn-faced NKVD officers.

Richter faced his interrogators below a single light bulb. The room seemed claustrophobic and very still. The Colonel sat behind a long wooden table, an empty notepad open in front of him. Cigarettes and an ash tray lay ready beside the pad.

'Name all the people you have been imprisoned with,' the Colonel demanded.

Richter closed his eyes for a moment. His mouth felt dry. He cleared his throat and coughed. He was thinking fast. Just what was this all about? What did they want?

He paused, and then began the directory of names, hesitating every few moments to be sure his memory had not skipped a name.

When Richter mentioned the name of Wallenberg, the Colonel stopped him.

Years later, Richter would relive that moment. 'They then asked me to give the names of all those to whom I had mentioned having met Wallenberg.'

As Richter talked, the Colonel made notes. He had found what he was looking for, and Richter was marched out of the interrogation room. He turned to head towards his cell, but the guard shuffled him down the corridor, past his own block and on to the punishment cells. For the next seven months, Richter was held in solitary confinement.

After Richter left the interrogation cell that night, the other foreign prisoners were marched in, one at a time, to face the Colonel. Loyda, Roedel, Scheur...

Every prisoner thought to have seen or talked to Raoul Wallenberg was interrogated that night. All were warned never to speak of Wallenberg. All were kept in solitary confinement for several months afterwards.

Horst Kitschmann testified, 'They asked me to name all the people I had shared cells with. When I mentioned Langfelder's name they asked me what he had told me. After I recounted what I had heard, the NKVD Colonel in charge asked me whom I had told about Langfelder.'

Kitschmann was taken from the interrogation cell and held in solitary confinement from that night, 27 July 1947, until 23 February 1948. When he asked his jailers why he was held in solitary, he was told it was 'a punishment for having told your cell-mates about Langfelder and Wallenberg'.

Another cellmate confirmed these events. Ernst Huber was also questioned that same night and asked to list the names of prisoners with whom he had been imprisoned. Huber recalls that the Colonel stopped when the list reached Langfelder. He said, 'The rest of the interrogation concerned Wallenberg and what Langfelder had told me about him.'

Like the others, Huber was held for several months in solitary confinement. The pattern was followed for every prisoner who had shared a cell with Wallenberg or his driver, Vilmos Langfelder.

Moscow – Stockholm, 1947

The interrogations of 27 July were part of the preparations as Russian policy on the case was being finalized. Nearly a month later, on 18 August 1947, the Soviet Foreign Minister, Andrei Vishinsky, fired a salvo in reply to continued Swedish enquiries into the mystery of Raoul Wallenberg.

Vishinsky's statement read, 'Wallenberg is not in the Soviet Union and is unknown to us.' The note concluded with the assumption that the missing diplomat had been killed in battle in Hungary or by fascists or Nazi gunmen. Ironically, the Soviet statement adhered closely to Soderblom's advice to Stalin in June 1946. This would remain official Soviet policy on the Raoul Wallenberg case for the next 10 years.

The news must have shocked Raoul's mother and stepfather, Maj and Fredrik von Dardel, his stepsister Nina Lagergren, and their family and friends in Stockholm, all of whom were eagerly awaiting the return of their beloved hero.

The news did not cause such a stir in the Foreign Office, however, and they still had not followed up any of the leads that the journalist Eduard af Sandeberg had produced. Nonetheless, following mounting pressure and press coverage, the Foreign Office now set up a committee to review evidence that was accumulating.

In November 1947, Foreign Minister Unden, a pro-Russian and prominent Marxist, met with members of Raoul's family and the Wallenberg Committee. When questioned repeatedly about Vishinsky's statement, Unden replied somewhat heatedly, 'What, do you believe that Mr Vishinsky is lying?'

'Yes,' replied one of the more outspoken members of the Committee.

Unden was clearly exasperated. 'This is incredible, absolutely incredible!' he repeated. Vishinsky had played a prominent role in Stalin's vicious purges and show trials in the 1930s, but Unden could not bring himself to question the integrity of the Russian leader.

While the Swedish Foreign Office raised the art of political boredom to fever pitch, the Jews of Budapest were preparing to honour Raoul's memory and commemorate his achievements. A statue was commissioned and in April 1948 the Mayor of Budapest, Josef Bognar, was set to honour the missing diplomat's mission. The night before the unveiling ceremony, however, the statue disappeared. It had been removed by Soviet soldiers and turned up two years later outside a state pharmaceutical factory in the eastern city of Debrecen, where it remained for several years. The plaque naming Wallenberg had been removed. The inscription had read, 'This memorial is our silent and eternal gratitude to him and should always remind us of his enduring humanity in a period of inhumanity.'

That same year, 1948, Raoul was recommended for the Nobel Peace Prize and Albert Einstein, among other dignitaries, supported the nomination.

The Russian response was swift and crushing. The *New Times*, a semi-official Soviet weekly, published an article on 'The Wallenberg Legend'. With no mention of his exploits in Hungary, Raoul was portrayed as an excuse for 'anti-Soviet provocation' caused by 'American warmongers'.

As the Russians had predicted, their note from Vishinsky effectively silenced the Swedes, who were in awe of the communist revolution and anxious not to antagonize their powerful neighbour.

The Russians must surely have been puzzled that no concerted or forceful attempt was made to extricate their diplomat from the living maze in which he was trapped. Clearly, this would have confirmed their suspicions of Raoul's crimes. He must be a spy! After all, what was he doing in Hungary at such a dangerous time? Saving Jewish lives? What an absurd cover that must have seemed.

According to some accounts, the Russians were interested in the possibility of an exchange. It had been worked to good advantage in other cases and was becoming standard diplomatic strategy. Early in 1946, the Swiss government had successfully negotiated the exchange of one of their citizens, Harold Feller, who had worked alongside Raoul in Budapest. There were striking parallels. At first, the Russians denied all knowledge of Feller's arrest while he was accused of spying. The Swiss refused to abandon efforts for his release and within a year, Feller was freed in exchange for eight Soviet citizens convicted of espionage. Feller was released along with four other Swiss diplomatic and consular officials.

A meeting in Moscow with the Swedish chargé d'affaires, Ulf Barck-Holst, and officials at the Foreign Ministry confirmed Russian interest in an exchange. When Barck-Holst raised the case of Wallenberg, an official replied, 'What information can you give us about Lydia Makarova, or Anatoly Granovsky or the Balts?' This revealed that the Russians had not ruled out the possibility of exchanging the missing diplomat. That decision was made in Sweden. The Marxist Foreign Minister Unden completely refused to discuss the possible exchange under any conditions.

Lefortovo Prison

Willi Bergemann, in cell 202, was next door to Raoul Wallenberg, in cell 203; immediately above and just to the right, in cell 105, was

Bernhard Rensinghoff. Both recall hearing a hasty message on the prison telegraph coming from Raoul's cell.

Tap! Tap! Tap! . . . We are being taken away. . .

Following this, they heard the sound of fists being pounded against the wall. The prisoners were removed and for the next few days the cell next door to Bergemann, which had once held Raoul Wallenberg, was silent, presumably empty. Both men are vague about the specific date of the incident; Rensinghoff thinks it was probably around the summer of 1946, while Bergemann places it sometime between March and May 1947.

Following Stalin's enquiry into Wallenberg, all prisoners who had come into contact with Raoul were isolated. The new rules also stipulated that Raoul was to be held in solitary confinement and, when he did share a cell, he was to be held with long-serving Russians only.

And so the incredibly lonely odyssey of Raoul Wallenberg had begun. Through the subterranean netherworld of the Gulag prison chain, Raoul was to be a silent witness. Over the next few years, hopes were dashed as the 'Welcome home, Raoul' signs faded. But in 1951, electrifying news forced Wallenberg back onto the agenda.

An Italian diplomat, recently exchanged from a Russian jail, happened to mention Raoul's name during a cocktail party to celebrate his release. The diplomat was Claudio de Mohr, and he had been in cell 152 in Lefortovo Prison – next door, he said, to a prisoner named Raoul Wallenberg.

Moscow – Stockholm, 1952–7

Eventually the news reached Raoul's mother in Stockholm through mutual friends. De Mohr's evidence spurred the Swedes to press the Russians on the case once again.

The Swedes first wrote in February 1952 and received a reply on 16 April. Nothing had changed. The Russians said, in effect,

'Who? Wallenberg? Never heard of him.' Not to be deterred, the Swedes made another attempt, one month later in May 1952. This time the Russians waited 15 months before replying. Soviet Ambassador Konstantin Rodionov stated, 'Wallenberg has not been and is not in the Soviet Union and is unknown to us.'

Between 1952 and 1954, the Swedes made 15 written and 34 oral requests to the Soviet Union for Wallenberg's return. The Soviet reply remained unchanged: 'Wallenberg has not been and is not in the Soviet Union and is unknown to us.'

In 1955 Konrad Adenauer, the West German Chancellor, successfully negotiated the release of German POWs from Russian captivity. Stirred by the Italian de Mohr's testimony, the Swedish Foreign Office were on the lookout for anyone with news of the missing diplomat. Stern investigative procedures were established.

Even the cautious Swedes must have been surprised at the outcome. The list was staggering. Suddenly Wallenberg's cellmates were in the West as free men. They began to talk.

'Yes, I knew Raoul Wallenberg. I shared a prison cell with Raoul in Lubyanka Prison...' It was Richter. Others followed.

Now, news of Raoul's arrest, imprisonment and captivity were beyond doubt. The evidence of these men proved conclusively that he had survived and that he was still alive. There was hope. This was 1955.

These devastating statements were provided by those who had communicated directly with Raoul Wallenberg. The interviews were eventually incorporated into a 'White Book' published by the Swedish Foreign Office.

Gustav Richter was first: 'During the time R.W. spent together with me in Lubyanka Prison, he was only questioned once. The inspector leading the examination said to him, among other things, "Well, you are well known to us. You belong to a great capitalist family in Sweden." R.W. was accused of espionage. The examination lasted about one-and-a-half hours. During the month we spent together, he kept his spirits up and was in a good mood.'

Karl Supprian: 'When I was first informed of the presence of a Swedish diplomat in the prison I was so surprised that I asked Roedel once more to confirm his report to avoid misunderstanding. Roedel repeated his information. Usually, I "knocked" directly to Roedel, but in some cases also to R.W.'

Ernst Wallenstein: 'Through these knockings, I learnt that R.W. had possessed a diplomatic passport, and that he had been commissioned by the Swedish government to help the Jews in Budapest. R.W. was arrested as being suspected of espionage, as he had been in a section occupied by the Russians.'

Heinz Helmut von Hinckeldey: 'I also had direct contact with R.W. My knockings with him were in German. In this way we exchanged addresses for example, and Wallenberg said that the bank firm Wallenberg in Stockholm was enough as an address for him.'

Willi Bergemann: 'R.W was a very eager knocker. He spoke and knocked fluent German. He called us by knocking five times in a row. During this time, I learnt about R.W. that on the 13th January 1945, he had gone to the Russian headquarters to negotiate with the Russians … on this occasion, R.W. was arrested and sent to Moscow suspected of espionage. While R.W. was in cell 203, he asked on repeated occasions to get information by the commissar about his fate.'

Bernhard Rensinghoff: 'The contact between me and the two in the cell above became most intensive. Every day we exchanged messages. Roedel as well as R.W. were eager knockers. In this way, R.W. told me about his activity in Budapest and about his being arrested. As his address, R.W. stated Stockholm. Our cell companion Josias von Rantzau told us about the Wallenbergs, whom he knew of from his time in Stockholm. During the first time our knocking connections were mostly used to compose a letter in French. In this letter R.W. referred to his diplomatic status and asked to be examined. R.W. had sent this letter to Stalin in summer 1946 with a request to get a chance of contacting the Swedish

Legation in Moscow. Concerning the choice of French words he asked among others Rantzau for advice. After some time, R.W. got a message in which the dispatch of his letter was confirmed.'

Ernst Wallenstein again: 'I still remember quite clearly about this, as R.W. had the intention to write a letter of protest and was not quite sure to whom he ought to send it. Through knockings we agreed that it would be best to send it to Stalin himself and that it should be written in French. I suggested to address Stalin as "*Monsieur le President*" and also suggested the polite phrase "*Agréez, Monsieur le President, l'expression de ma très haute consideration*." I know that R.W. wrote such a letter and had it sent away by the guard.'

Details of the arrest in Budapest emerged from Erhard Hille, who had shared cell 105 in Lubyanka Prison with Vilmos Langfelder. Hille stated, 'After the Russian conquest of the city R.W. wished to contact the Russian headquarters to get protection for the Jews. R.W. and Langfelder drove off alone in a car. As there still were frequent bombardments in the streets, they had to move forwards very slowly and hide now and then in different houses. After some time they were stopped by some Russian soldiers, who forced them to get out of the car. The tyres were cut in pieces. R.W. showed his legitimation and asked to be brought to the chief commandant. Instead they were brought to NKVD and sat for some time in a provisory NKVD prison in Budapest. After that they were brought by one officer and four soldiers to Moscow. In Budapest as well as in Moscow they were told that they were not considered prisoners but that they were to be put in preventive custody. In Moscow they had been shown the underground railway among other things and they had walked to Lubyanka Prison. Langfelder had not seen R.W. since then.'

There were minor inconsistencies about dates and times, but the essential details confirmed the fact: Wallenberg had survived.

From the ex-POWs' testimony, the Swedish government learned important information about Raoul's arrest and imprisonment inside Russia. They also learned of the sinister interrogation and isolation of foreign prisoners who had shared cells with Wallenberg, which had taken place on 27 July 1947. They recognized that Soviet tactics had changed since that night. The date was significant and the tactics were designed to prevent information on Wallenberg from spreading.

Bolstered by such stunning evidence, what strategy did the Swedes deploy?

Playing postman, a Swedish courier delivered a note to the Soviet Foreign Ministry. 'Complete evidence' was in the hands of the Swedish government, the Kremlin was told, which confirmed that Wallenberg was alive and lost in a Soviet prison. Not to be deterred, the Swedes were marshalling themselves for yet another assault. This time, it was to be a declaration from the Swedish Supreme Court of Justice.

Did these actions have any effect on the case?

Nyet!

On 5 April 1956, the Russians stated that the case was under review. On 14 July that year, the Soviet Ambassador Rodionov confirmed that the results of a new Soviet investigation would be released 'shortly'.

Confronted with the evidence of reliable witnesses who were free to testify at an independent tribunal, the Soviets shuffled their cards. The Swedes sat back, calm and dignified. Raoul's family dared to hope.

Moscow – Stockholm, 2 February 1957

No one could have been prepared for the Soviet reply. It was crushing in its finality. Delivered on 2 February 1957 by Andrei Gromyko, Deputy Foreign Minister, the reply read:

> In pursuance of the Swedish Government's request, the Soviet Government instructed the pertinent Soviet authorities to pursue the material concerning Raoul Wallenberg...

In this connection, the competent Soviet authorities have undertaken to search page by page the archive documents from all wards in certain prisons. As a result of such search of archive documents from the health service in the Lubyanka Prison, a document has been found which there is good reason to consider as referring to Raoul Wallenberg.

This document has the form of a handwritten report, addressed to the former minister of state security of the Soviet Union, Abakumov, and written in the hand of the health service director of said prison, A. I. Smoltsov, reading as follows:

I report that the prisoner Walenberg [sic], who is well known to you, died suddenly in his cell last night, probably as the result of a heart attack.'

Abakumov, the minister in question, was dead and no witnesses could testify. The note itself was not produced, nor even a photocopy of it. The date of Wallenberg's 'death' is remarkably close to the date when all prisoners in contact with Raoul were questioned and then isolated to stop information about him from spreading.

The Swedes' sluggish mishandling – almost bungling – of the case had now taken a dramatic twist. The Kremlin had closed their file on Raoul Wallenberg. The case was complete. Gromyko, that long-time political survivor, had put his name to it. The Swedes, acting in character, followed this devastating news with a diplomatic note 'strongly regretting' the news.

Nikita Khrushchev, the new Soviet leader, had now become the focus of attention for the Swedish authorities. On an official visit to Sweden, in June 1964, he was again pressed on the Wallenberg case.

On the day Khrushchev arrived in Stockholm, the influential Swedish newspaper, *Expressen*, carried this front-page headline: 'QUESTION: WHERE IS RAOUL WALLENBERG?' The article addressed Khrushchev directly: 'You arrive empty handed.

' Soviet statement made by Andrei Gromyko, 2 February 1957. See Appendix 2.

Even though you may have 50 people in your entourage, the number is incomplete, if Raoul Wallenberg is not one of them. Whatever gifts you may have brought, it is not enough, if you don't have Raoul Wallenberg.'

Premier Nikolai Bulganin, accompanying Khrushchev on the visit, was furious when the case was raised by the new Swedish Prime Minister, Tage Erlander. 'This is a waste of time. We don't have time for this nonsense,' Bulganin declared.

Chapter 15

◥◣

BURIED ALIVE

Gulag, 1948–?

Wallenberg had been buried alive in a prison cell in the heart of Soviet Russia. The prison door had swung shut, the key had been tossed away. A living man had been declared dead. Yet the corpse just would not lie still.

As foreign POWs returned to the West, tantalizing titbits of information and tales of unexpected encounters with the missing diplomat were reported. With the passing of time, one nugget of truth remained uncovered: Wallenberg had outlived his death in prison.

In the summer of 1948, Dr Menachem Meltzer, an Austrian Jew, claimed that he had examined a Swedish prisoner in a camp called Khalimer Yu in the far north. When asked to identify himself, the Swede replied, 'My name is Raoul'.

By the 1950s, Wallenberg had been moved to Vladimir Prison and once again the sightings began. A Swiss prisoner named Brugger returned home to reveal that he had been next door to the missing diplomat. During their first exchange of communication, Brugger's neighbour introduced himself: 'Wallenberg, First Secretary, Swedish Legation, Budapest, arrested 1945.' Wallenberg asked Brugger to go to any Swedish Embassy and report his case. He told Brugger that he was not allowed to write letters or to receive mail. Brugger, like Wallenberg, had never been tried or sentenced.

At Vladimir Prison, Abraham Kalinski heard of Wallenberg in 1951 from David Vandrovsky, a Jewish author who had shared a cell with Raoul. Wallenberg had spoken about his arrest in Budapest and said that he had been accused of spying. Two years later, Kalinski saw Wallenberg exercising in the prison yard and in January 1955 he travelled on the same train as Raoul during a prison transfer.

Kalinski shared a cell with Simon Gogoberidse, a Georgian Social Democrat who had been kidnapped from Paris by the KGB. Gogoberidse told Kalinski that he had shared a cell with Wallenberg, who was only held with prisoners serving very lengthy sentences like himself.

In a postcard dated October 1959 addressed to his sister in Haifa, Kalinski wrote, 'Have met a Swede who saved the Jews of Romania.'

Kalinski reported that Wallenberg was held in cell 23 in solitary confinement in Vladimir Prison.

While in Vladimir Prison, Wallenberg met an Austrian who cannot be identified for fear of reprisals. This man talked at length to Raoul, who told him he had spent years in solitary confinement. As they parted, Raoul urged the Austrian to contact any Swedish Mission if he was released. Raoul said, 'If you forget my name, just say "a Swede from Budapest", and they'll know who you mean.' The Austrian was removed the following day and warned not to speak about the encounter with Wallenberg, or he could receive life imprisonment.

Moscow, 1961

The sixties saw the greatest chance of solving the mystery of the missing diplomat. It came unexpectedly when a prominent physician, Professor Nanna Svartz, a close friend of the von Dardel family, had a routine meeting in Moscow on 27 January 1961 with a colleague, Professor Aleksandr Miashnikov. As usual, they communicated in German, a shared language.

While they talked, Dr Svartz explained her interest in Raoul Wallenberg and asked the Russian professor if he had any knowledge of this case. Beyond her wildest hopes, the professor replied that he knew the case well. Speaking in a low voice, Dr Miashnikov stated that he himself had personally examined Raoul, who was currently in a psychiatric hospital.

The news was relayed to the Swedish Prime Minister, Tage Erlander, who sent Khrushchev a personal letter the following month outlining these new developments. In March 1961 Professor Svartz returned to Moscow, but was startled by Miashnikov's response, as he strongly reprimanded her for her action.

As chairman to Khrushchev's personal physician, he had held a prominent position in the Kremlin's hierarchy. Miashnikov said that after Erlander's letter was received, he was summoned to Khrushchev's office. The Russian premier was furious and slammed his fist on the desk, cursed Miashnikov for speaking of Wallenberg and finally ordered the professor out of his office. Miashnikov disclaimed any further information on Wallenberg and later recanted his original statement about knowing the Swede.

Two years later, in 1963, ex-British spy Greville Wynne had an unusual encounter in Moscow's Lubyanka Prison. One day, when he was being taken in the tiny, cage-like lift to the roof for solitary exercise, Wynne heard another cage coming into the next pen. As the gate opened, a voice called out, 'Taxi!' Given the filthy conditions of the lifts, this piece of defiant humour was greatly appreciated. Five days later, when it happened again, Wynne called out, 'Are you American?' The voice answered, 'No, I'm Swedish.' Before anything further could be exchanged, however, the guards restrained both prisoners.

In 1980, when the Wallenberg story hit the headlines in America, Dr Marvin Makinen, a physicist at the University of Chicago, recalled his own experiences in Vladimir Prison. Makinen was arrested for espionage in Kiev and served three years of an eight-year sentence in Soviet prisons between 1961 and 1964. He was in

Vladimir Prison at the same time as Francis Gary Powers, who had been arrested after his U-2 spy plane had been shot down by the Russians. Powers was exchanged for Russian agent Rudolf Abel in 1962, and Makinen was moved into his cell in Vladimir, inheriting Zygurd Kruminsh as a cellmate. Makinen was suspicious of Kruminsh and thought him to be a KGB informer. Later a fellow prisoner said of Kruminsh, 'He got to sit with all the foreigners – with you, with Powers and with the Swede, van den Berg.'

When Makinen was exchanged in 1964, he was debriefed in Washington and related his account about Kruminsch and the Swede. He was asked to repeat the story to the Swedish Embassy in Washington, which he did. One year later he was asked to tell his story again to two representatives of the Swedish Embassy. After he had finished, Makinen was apparently told not to repeat the story elsewhere.

When Makinen heard about Raoul through the news media, he realized that 'the Swede, van den Berg' was possibly Wallenberg, as 'W' is frequently pronounced 'V' by non-English-speaking people, including the Swedes. Makinen telephoned the Wallenberg family in Sweden with this information and was surprised to learn that the Swedish Embassy had never passed this news on to the von Dardel family.

In 1973, Haim Moshinski, in a sworn affidavit from his home in Israel, gave evidence to a US House of Representatives Investigating Committee claiming he had seen Wallenberg in a notorious camp at Wrangel Island in 1962. Moshinski described Wallenberg as a 'handsome, educated man'.

Others also reported seeing Wallenberg at Wrangel Island, a tiny patch of icy ground located 300 miles inside the Arctic Circle, 80 miles northeast of Siberia. Wrangel Island had apparently held camps for secret agents and long-serving prisoners. Rumours abound of human experiments being conducted there.

While it is easy to dismiss this as a James Bond fantasy, an incredible incident confirmed that someone in that region was desperately trying to communicate with the outside world. In 1971, an Italian hunter shot down a goose. A rubber tube was attached to it containing a scrap of paper. The paper had faded and the words were barely distinguishable. It read, 'SOS ... Italian officers ... island beyond the Arctic Circle.'

Around this time a Hungarian-born prisoner claimed he met Raoul in a camp for foreigners in Irkutsk, near Lake Baikal in the south. Wallenberg allegedly told the Hungarian he had just been transported there from Wrangel Island. Wallenberg apparently shared a two-room wooden shack with Aleksandr Trushnovich, the leader of the Russian émigré group NTS, who had been abducted from Berlin. Their food was delivered by an Italian named Pelgrini, whom Raoul approached about smuggling information out of the camp.

Moscow, 1979

Years after his arrest, the footprints of Wallenberg's journey can be traced through the seventies.

Simon Wisenthal, the celebrated Nazi-hunter, took a personal interest in the case following a plea from Maj von Dardel, Raoul's mother. Wisenthal uncovered the evidence of General Kuprianov, who had been held in a Soviet prison and had seen Raoul between 1953 and 1956.

In 1979, when news of Kuprianov's meeting with Wallenberg was printed in a Russian émigré newspaper, the Russian General was interrogated by the KGB and ordered to 'refute American provocations'.

Apparently General Kuprianov became fearful. 'I do not know if I will be able to manage that questioning.' The KGB picked Kuprianov up again and five days later his wife was told that he had died of a heart attack. While she was at the centre claiming the body, their apartment was searched and all the General's papers and documents were removed.

One witness may have vanished, but another emerged. Jan Kaplan, a former administrator of an operatic studio in Moscow, was released from prison in 1977. One of his first acts as a free man was to phone his daughter, Anna Bilder, in Jaffa, Israel.

When asked about prison life and the harsh conditions, Kaplan told his daughter that things were not too difficult. He explained, 'Why, when I was in Butyrki Prison Hospital in 1975, I met a Swede who told me he had been in Soviet prisons for 30 years and he seemed reasonably healthy to me.' Was this merely a throwaway comment to his daughter, or was Kaplan trying to send out a secret message on behalf of Raoul?

Anna Bilder was unaware of the importance of what she had learned, but eventually she reported her story to the Swedish Foreign Office and as a result Sweden officially reopened the Wallenberg case. A fresh enquiry was sent to the Soviets on 3 January 1979.

One month after the Swedish query, on 3 February 1979, the Kaplan home in Moscow was searched and Jan Kaplan was re-arrested. He was 66 at the time. In Israel, Anna Bilder received three anonymous calls, two of them in Russian. She was warned not to speak of Wallenberg again for the sake of her father.

In June that year, Anna Bilder received a note from her mother, Eugenia Kaplan, in Moscow, stating that Jan was arrested because he had tried to smuggle out a letter about Wallenberg.

When Eugenia Kaplan visited her husband in Lubyanka Prison, the KGB Colonel in charge of the investigation warned her that Jan Kaplan's fate depended on Anna Bilder's behaviour. The Kaplan family decided they could play no further role in the Wallenberg affair.

Confirmation of Kaplan's news came from another quarter, however. A young Russian Jewish immigrant to Israel told a remarkable story. He wished to remain anonymous because his family still lived in the USSR. The young Russian had never heard of Wallenberg until he settled in Israel. He went immediately to the Swedish Embassy in Israel and told them of a party at the Moscow home of a senior KGB officer on May Day, 1978. 'Much vodka was drunk,' he said, 'and the younger men at the party began to speak of dissidents and the rough time they must have in prison. The KGB officer burst out and said, "Don't you believe it. Things aren't so tough nowadays as they used to be. You can live a long time in jail. Why, I have a Swede under my charge in Lubyanka who's been inside for over 30 years!"'

Chapter 16

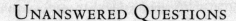

UNANSWERED QUESTIONS

Why would the Russians continue to imprison Raoul Wallenberg?

Dr Gideon Hausner, Eichmann's prosecutor and chairman of Yad Vashem's Council, was clear: 'The Soviets just couldn't believe that a Swedish diplomat would dedicate himself for months to this job of rescuing Jews. To them it must have looked a very silly and unconvincing cover for other activities.'

Clearly, Wallenberg must have been viewed as a bizarre figure in the ruins of Budapest, with sackfuls of money and valuables, forged documents, hundreds of passports, underworld contacts. A rogue adventurer busily bribing officials, linked to the black market, consorting with Nazis and Arrow Cross fascists as well as the resistance, while fake Swedish passports bearing his signature appeared everywhere.

Presumably he explained his American connections during his interrogations, and Russian intelligence would have 'decoded' this connection. If Wallenberg was backed by the OSS, the forerunner of the CIA, then naturally he must be a spy.

The NKVD (KGB) controlled the arrest but allowed it to remain theatrical. Raoul himself was troubled, but ready to believe the best. He suspected that things were not right. 'I don't know if I'm their guest or their prisoner,' he had commented, referring to his Russian escort.

The NKVD functioned as a state within a state and was probably acting under special instructions. It has emerged that the order to detain Wallenberg in Hungary was signed by Bulganin. A decade later, in 1957, Bulganin was the Soviet premier when the final declaration of Wallenberg's 'death in 1947' was issued.

What is overwhelmingly certain is that the Russians suspected Wallenberg of being a spy. During his interrogation in Moscow, Raoul was told that he had been imprisoned because he was a spy, that he would never be officially charged, nor would he ever stand trial. The interrogating officer said, 'For political reasons, you will never be tried.' This information has been confirmed by released POWs.

Lars Berg and Gote Carlsson, diplomats at the Swedish Legation in Hungary, were similarly accused of being spies during their own interrogations by the NKVD. When the Swedes explained their mission and confirmed Raoul's role in Hungary, the NKVD officers flatly refused to believe what they said.

Many of Wallenberg's colleagues were interrogated and accused of spying. Each of them was questioned about Raoul's real role in Hungary.

Paul Hegedus was held for intense questioning during the month of February 1945. The NKVD officer in charge shouted, 'We know the entire Swedish Legation here in Hungary were spying.' When Hegedus repeated that Raoul's mission in Hungary was simply to rescue Jews, the Russian officer roared with laughter.

Waldemar Langlet, the Swedish Red Cross representative in Budapest, and his wife, who both worked alongside Raoul, were also detained for questioning by the NKVD.

Lars Berg and Per Anger, Raoul's colleagues in Budapest, have spoken about the 'spy threat'. Berg was taken into custody and interrogated. The Soviets refused to believe that the Swedish Mission was involved in any such humanitarian efforts to aid Jews. He was also accused of fabricating false documents for non-Jews and was repeatedly asked, 'Why would Berg and Wallenberg, neutrals and Christians, risk their lives for Jews?'

In a BBC TV interview, Berg asserted, 'My opinion is this: that Wallenberg told them that he wasn't only a Swedish diplomat, but he was sent by President Roosevelt himself. He was working with American money to save Jewish lives. I think that's why he disappeared, that it wasn't good at that time to declare that you worked for the Americans.'

The Soviets must have been suspicious about Sweden's lackadaisical attitude to Wallenberg's imprisonment. If what he said was true, why had he been abandoned by his own people? No doubt they asked him that time and again. The question must have stunned Raoul. Why indeed?

Those who should have done the most did the least. The diplomatic efforts on his behalf have been distinguished by their ineptness and apathy. To this day there has never been a concerted, convincing and combined effort to win his freedom.

The case also suffered from a tragic lack of international public awareness. For 30 years, the Wallenberg story was known in just four places: in Sweden, where he is a cause célèbre, in Hungary, in Israel and, of course, in the Soviet Union.

The Soviets indicated on several occasions that they would consider an exchange deal, but the Swedes vetoed the idea until it was too late. Worse, the Soviets may have expected it. When such a deal did not transpire, it would have justified their earlier suspicions about espionage. Some have claimed that the Russians offered a swap in 1968.

Throughout the first two decades of Wallenberg's imprisonment, several other countries concluded successful deals with the Soviets and obtained the release of their countrymen. It was these ex-POWs who brought out testimony about the one who remained behind.

Harold Feller, a Swiss diplomat who worked alongside Raoul in Budapest, also disappeared in the same year, 1945. The Soviets at first denied all knowledge of him, but the Swiss government persisted and within a year had negotiated his release via a prisoner exchange.

In October 1981, the Swedes were pressed to hold onto a Soviet submarine that ran aground while in Swedish territorial waters. The Swedish Foreign Minister considered the potential of an exchange – the submarine for Wallenberg – as an 'unethical act'.

Per Anger was clearly frustrated that his own government had not done more. He told the BBC, 'With the Soviets you have to offer something.' The Swedes had Soviet spies after the war, he said, but they were expelled. 'We could have held them in prison until we had got Wallenberg back, but it wasn't within their vocabulary, this way of acting.'

Wallenberg's name may have impressed his American selectors when they were choosing him for the mission in Budapest, but in a KGB interrogation cell the name proved devastating.

The Russians had not forgotten Sweden's role in the war and were convinced that the war had been prolonged because of the vital ore deliveries that kept being exported to Germany from Swedish companies. Russian officers had accused Ivan Danielsson, the Swedish Minister in Hungary, of this. And who had been instrumental in controlling the trade? The Wallenberg dynasty.

Jacob Wallenberg co-ordinated trade with the Germans, while Marcus Wallenberg dealt with the Allies. In his book entitled *Pack of Thieves*, Richard Chesnoff notes that Swedish industrial giants supplied the Germans with parts for the engines used in the deadly v-2 rockets that blitzed Allied ships and cities, but also provided the Allies with ball bearings flown out of Sweden in the RAF's Mosquito aircraft. Chesnoff confirms that, of all the neutral countries, Sweden was the most helpful to the Nazis. During the war, Sweden granted Germany significant transit rights across its territory, permitting more than 250,000 trips by German troops across this neutral land to reach Finland. The focus of the operation was to combat Soviet occupation forces.

Chesnoff cites the US government's 1998 Eizenstat Report: 'It was a generally held view among Allied economic warfare experts early in the war that the German war effort depended on iron ore from Sweden and oil from the Soviet Union and that without these materials, the war would come to a halt.'

Chesnoff's important study details how the Nazis systematically looted the Jews of Europe and reveals the sinister role played by most European nations. He calls it 'the largest organized robbery in history'. The story parallels the accusation that Swiss banks were still hoarding the assets of Holocaust victims.

At the nerve centre of all this financial activity were the Wallenbergs, who controlled the most influential bank in Sweden. Today, the Wallenberg holding company is considered to control more than 40 per cent of the value of the entire Swedish stock exchange.

Dutch historians Gerard Aalders and Cees Wiebes have documented how the Wallenbergs assisted the Reichsbank in bypassing American embargoes on trade with Nazi Germany. In addition, huge quantities of valuables plundered by the Nazis from their Jewish victims and amassed in Hungary were transferred to Sweden at the end of the war. Banks controlled by the Wallenberg family apparently laundered the funds. The Wallenberg banks also became a significant conduit for laundering the loot of individual Nazis, especially from Hungary.

One of the most audacious cloaking schemes between the Nazis and the Wallenbergs concerned the 'acquisition' of the America Bosch Corporation (ABC), a US subsidiary of the Nazi Germany firm Robert Bosch GmbH. The Wallenbergs had allegedly agreed to return ABC to the Nazis after the war had ended with a German victory.

The Wallenbergs' policy was not always in favour of the Soviets. At one time they entered into a secret deal with the US to block trade with the USSR. One report claims that the Americans blocked the Wallenbergs' assets in the US. The block was apparently only lifted when the Wallenbergs agreed to sabotage Swedish credit to the Soviet Union and to co-operate in the American embargo policy towards Moscow.

These shady, backwater dealings were alleged by G. Adler Karlsson in *Western Economic Warfare*, published in English in Sweden. In a footnote (on page 244) he writes:

> According to information from Swedish top diplomats at the relevant time there was one more reason for the difficulties of the Soviet Union to import from Sweden, namely a conscious policy by the so-called Wallenberg group not to sell. This policy was not based only on the general threat of commercial repercussions, but was based on a special event, concerning wartime transactions of the Wallenberg group with the German Bosch interests.

If this anti-Soviet trade policy, manipulated by the US and manoeuvred by the Wallenbergs in Sweden, was true, this secret deal would naturally have infuriated the Russians. When they realized that they actually had in their custody one of the members of the Wallenberg family, and he was enjoying the hospitality of the State...

At his first interview in Lubyanka Prison the secret police greeted Raoul with the words, 'Ah, yes, Mr Wallenberg. We know all about you. You are from a big, capitalist family in Sweden.'

Despite some gestures, the Wallenbergs in Sweden did pitifully little to aid their cousin. In 1979, a BBC TV crew were refused entry to film inside the bank building. This was for a documentary on Raoul, the first international broadcast about him.

It is likely that Raoul had details of Jewish assets. Did the Russians pressure him to turn this information over to them? And what happened to the large amount of money and valuables that Raoul was carrying with him at the time of his disappearance? There is no record of the Swedish government ever asking the Soviets for an explanation.

The Soviets would have been aware of Marcus and Jacob Wallenberg's diverse but devious roles during the war years. Perhaps they realized that the opportunity for revenge or blackmail presented itself. After all, they had Raoul locked up in the cellar. They might have considered him an important asset to be used to influence decisions with his powerful uncles in Sweden. It is hard to imagine that the name Wallenberg played no part in his disappearance.

Could Wallenberg have been a spy?

Conspiracy theories abound, with many diverse tangents. Some question whether or not Wallenberg may have been a secret Russian agent. He easily fits the mould after all, coming from the same upper-class background and holding the same liberal attitudes as the 'Apostles' in Cambridge. The Apostles Society in Cambridge was an elite club of intellectuals, many of whom were left-wing. The most notorious British spies from this group included Philby, Burgess, Maclean and Blunt.

If Wallenberg was a Russian agent, it would explain why he was so insistent on contacting the Red Army at Debrecen. NKVD officers in Budapest were also on the lookout for him and possibly identified him from a photograph. While in custody in Moscow, Raoul apparently told one of his interrogators that he had 'looked after their [Soviet] interests in Budapest'. This is included in the evidence given by prisoners who returned to the West, and is included in the Swedish Foreign Office White Book on Raoul Wallenberg. The POWs stated that they heard this information from Wallenberg himself on the prison telegraph.

Why didn't people help?

For the bureaucrats, the Wallenberg case was a diplomatic mine-field.

The first tragic error had occurred when Sweden's Ambassador Soderblom refused America's offer of help. Soderblom's astonishing meeting with Stalin was also instrumental in sealing Wallenberg's fate. Both serious mistakes remained official secrets for many decades.

The pro-Marxist Foreign Minister Osten Unden clearly felt embarrassed by the case and wished it would simply go away. He was ready, almost eager, to accept any Soviet reply as the final word on the subject.

Curiously, other prominent Swedes were also reluctant to help.

Carl-Frederick Palmstierna, a friend of Raoul's mother, was private secretary to King Gustav VI between 1951 and 1973. King Gustav let it be known that he would not question Unden's handling of the situation.

In 1959, when Palmstierna tried once again to raise the Wallenberg case, the King became annoyed. 'What do you expect me to do?' he demanded. 'Are we supposed to ransack the prisons of Russia or declare war for the sake of Wallenberg?'

Palmstierna tried in vain to enlist the support of Dag Hammarskjöld when he became head of the United Nations in 1953. As a Swede, Hammarskjöld felt it was 'difficult for him to put the case of a compatriot to the Russians'. Palmstierna reflected that, if the issue had concerned a non-Swede, Hammarskjöld would probably have felt he had no right to meddle with internal questions involving other countries.

Raoul's mother approached Henry Kissinger in 1973 and an aide prepared a confidential memo on the subject dated 21 August 1973. All that was needed was Kissinger's signature to enable the United States officially to reopen the Wallenberg case after all those years. Kissinger never signed the document.

In a television interview in 1981, Kissinger explained, 'I took up the case of Wallenberg with Dobrynin [Soviet Ambassador to Washington] privately and was told Wallenberg was dead.' Clearly, the Russian Ambassador was not going to refute official Soviet policy overnight.

Curiously, on another occasion Kissinger gave a different explanation for not having signed the document. He told Lena Biork-Kaplan, of the American Free Wallenberg Committee, that he had never seen the memorandum and that it must have been disposed of by a subordinate. The memorandum, however, contains the notation 'Rejected by Kissinger, 10.15.1973'.

Sceptics have observed that relations between America and Sweden reached their lowest point in 1973, when Swedish Prime Minister Olof Palme had aroused Kissinger's anger by his criticism of US involvement in Vietnam, and in particular of President Richard Nixon's unauthorized bombing of Cambodia. How tragic, that by speaking out against atrocities in Southeast Asia the Swedes had unwittingly destroyed one of the last possible hopes of saving Wallenberg.

In February 1945, the Soviet Ambassador in Stockholm had told Raoul's mother and the wife of the Swedish Foreign Minister that Wallenberg would return and it would be better 'not to make a fuss'. Advocates of 'quiet diplomacy' would probably have endorsed that tactical strategy. Everything to do with Wallenberg's case was kept deafeningly silent and under wraps. By following this advice, however, initiatives were lost and years went by. Public outrage could not be focused into any cohesive campaign. Swedish newspapers considered this a 'betrayal'.

Today, the extraordinary story of Raoul Wallenberg is better known through international media coverage, newspaper articles, books, TV documentaries, dramas, and the internet.

In 1981, America bestowed its highest honour on Raoul Wallenberg and confirmed him as an honorary US citizen. In Israel, President Chaim Herzog also awarded him honorary citizenship, making Wallenberg the first to receive it under a law passed in March 1985. In Britain, David Amess MP launched a private member's bill in 1989 to give Raoul British citizenship. A decade later, the Queen of England unveiled a statue in London, marking his memory at a ceremony attended by the President of Israel.

Yet despite this recognition, the truth about Raoul Wallenberg's fate is still shrouded in mystery.

Could Wallenberg have survived?

It is not impossible!

Spartan conditions can be beneficial to a long life. A Japanese soldier lived in dense Philippine jungles for several years believing the war was still continuing.

While the Nazis executed their enemies, the communists banished theirs to the Gulag prison camps. During his research for the BBC documentary on Wallenberg, John Bierman met a Russian Jew called Leonid Berger, who was allowed to emigrate in 1978 after spending no fewer than 35 years in jails and camps.

Ivan Stepanov was continuously imprisoned from 1944 onwards. Ivan was born on 15 June 1930 and served over 40 years in jail. In 1983 former British Prime Minister Jim Callaghan carried an appeal for him to Moscow.

In 1986, an astonishing story emerged from Moscow confirming that a French POW was still alive in Russia after he disappeared when the Red Army swept Poland in 1945.

Early in March 1986, the Russians gave permission to the French Embassy in Moscow to make contact with Paul Catrain, a member of the 43rd French Artillery Regiment, who was 25 at the time of his disappearance. Catrain was missing, presumed dead, and his name is inscribed on the war memorial at Bois les Pargny, near Lyons in northeastern France. In truth, the French soldier was picked up by victorious Russian troops, together with many other soldiers of all nationalities, and was transferred to a POW camp in the Soviet Union. Since then, his tragic journey through the Gulag included time at a camp at Starokonstantinov in the Ukraine.

Patrick Meney, a French journalist who investigated the case, claimed that 600 Frenchmen had been held in Russia against their will during the years 1939 to 1945. Other sources indicated that there were 23 bona fide French families who requested repatriation.

Perhaps the most extraordinary survival story surfaced in July 2000, when a Hungarian named Andras Toma, aged 75, was found alive after 53 years in a psychiatric hospital outside Moscow. Toma was thought to have died on the Russian front in World War II. He was, in fact, captured by Russian troops in 1945 and hospital records show that Mr Toma was admitted to the institution in 1947. He has no clear memory of what happened and can barely speak Hungarian.

According to a report in *The Times*, about 1,000 elderly Koreans returned home in the spring of 2000. They had been sent by the Japanese to camps on the remote Far Eastern island of Sakhalin and were stranded there when the island became part of the Soviet empire after World War II. The paper also indicated that the Pentagon had documentation to suggest that American airmen shot down during the Korean War had worked and died in labour camps in central Siberia.

Wallenberg was not the only victim of the Red Army's liberation. Following their victory in Romania, Count Nikolai Tolstoy reports that about 320,000 Romanian soldiers were taken prisoner, 130,000 of whom were captured after hostilities ended. Also 100,000 more were enrolled into the Hungarian Army. Out of this total number of 420,000 people, only 190,000 returned home. In February 1945, Soviet authorities admitted that 50,000 had already died of undefined causes. The remaining 180,000 had been swallowed up into the ever-hungry belly of the Gulag system.

In *Stalin's Secret War*, Tolstoy states, 'Hungary's turn came next. Some 600,000 people were abducted by the NKVD and disappeared eastwards. They included many of the prisoners "liberated" from Auschwitz, Buchenwald and Ravensbruck, and almost the entire Hungarian population of Ruthenia, which province was intended in name as well as fact to join the other free republics of the USSR.'

The Soviets tried to keep Wallenberg in isolation. Those who saw him were warned not to speak of him. He was carefully guarded to limit contact. But from 27 July 1947, Soviet strategy changed.

While he was considered a spy, he was told he would not be charged for 'political reasons'. To some analysts, this signifies that prominent figures such as Leonid Brezhnev were complicit in his detention. Equally damaging was the participation of Andrei Gromyko, a long-time survivor of Russian politics. He put his name to the statement about Wallenberg's death in July 1947, but consistently refused to comment on this publicly.

The Brezhnev connection first emerged in 1981 when Yaakov Menaker, a former Soviet Army officer, emigrated to Israel and claimed that the future Soviet leader had ordered Wallenberg's arrest back in 1945. Menaker told the Swedish tabloid newspaper *Aftonbladet* that he had met several of the officers involved in the abduction at army veterans' meetings in the Soviet Union. Wallenberg's arrest was referred to as a 'secret successful operation'.

'Everybody was very careful about this. They knew it was a sensitive matter since it was connected with the 18th Army and everybody knew Brezhnev was in command of the unit,' Menaker explained.

The *International Herald Tribune* (10 August 1981) confirmed that Brezhnev was with the Soviet 18th Army in Hungary and revealed that a Swedish Supreme Court Justice knew of his involvement in the arrest. Ingrid Gaerde Widemaer told the domestic news agency TT, 'We have known since last fall that Brezhnev personally ordered the arrest of Raoul Wallenberg in Budapest in 1945 when he was Soviet Red Army *politruk*. Our big problem was whether we should make this public or not. We decided to keep silent in order not to jeopardize our efforts to seek Wallenberg's release.'

Four years later, in 1985, 40 years after his arrest, a new witness made a sensational claim: Raoul had fallen prey to Leonid Brezhnev's passion for foreign cars. The information was revealed in a letter, dated 9 June 1984, from a Ukrainian Catholic activist called Yosyp Terelia, and was published in the samizdat journal *A Chronicle of the Catholic Church in Ukraine.*

Terelia had been asked by his aunt, a Hungarian called Anna Maiorenko who knew the Swedish diplomat in Budapest, to make enquiries. Terelia's aunt had married Jyulo Siklo, an employee and a shareholder in the Hungarian National Bank in Budapest, who became involved in Wallenberg's rescue mission. They were active members of the Greek Catholic Church in Budapest and were planning church services to celebrate the new year. Raoul had been given a special invitation and on 9 January 1945, he telephoned to say he would attend the church meeting on 14 January – but on the night itself he was absent. By that time, he was already in Soviet hands.

Terelia's contact revealed the Brezhnev connection after becoming a Christian and confessing to his priest that he had witnessed the arrest.

Mr Terelia's letter also includes an account of his meeting in the Sychevskaya Special Psychiatric Hospital in 1973 with a Lithuanian named Bogdanas, a German citizen, who claimed to have met Wallenberg. The letter states:

During the war, Bogdanas had been an officer in the Wehrmacht. In 1945, he was arrested by Soviet counter intelligence and imprisoned in a camp that contained only foreigners. This was in the Norilsk labour camp complex. There Bogdanas met Wallenberg. For many years after this their fates seemed to be inseparably intertwined. In 1951, after the Norilsk uprising, all foreigners who were still alive were transferred to a small sixth zone. Of 8,000 people, only 420 were still alive.

In 1953, Wallenberg and Bogdanas were sent to a special psychiatric hospital in Kazan. In the hospital they began to 'cure Wallenberg of himself' – he was diagnosed as suffering from a 'mania of grandeur, he thinks he is a Swedish diplomat'.

Terelia also speculated about the risks he faced when writing of Wallenberg's arrest:

> Two daughters have been born in my absence [he had already spent many years in prison as a Catholic activist]. Obviously, the Soviet authorities will now arrest me again. And my third child who will come into the world in two months' time, will not see me. They know how to take their revenge. This letter is my death cry. I can feel it. They did not threaten me, no, they warned me: 'Don't concern yourself with Wallenberg. Keep your nose out of other people's business and we won't touch you. Keep quiet!'

The letter continues, 'It is difficult to say what will become of me and of my wife and children. The gauntlet has been thrown down. God is with us.'

On 20 August 1985, Yosyp Terelia was sentenced to 12 years in a labour camp and exile. His wife Alena, although qualified as a doctor, was unable to obtain work and was constantly harassed and pressurized because of her husband's activities.

Terelia was accused of 'anti-Soviet agitation and propaganda', an umbrella phrase that could mean almost anything. Clearly, Terelia knew how much danger he was in, but believed the truth was more important than any personal consequences. Forty years after Wallenberg's arrest, the Soviets still feared him.

Chapter 17

◼◼◼

WOULD GLASNOST MAKE
ANY DIFFERENCE?

Raoul's mother Maj refused to believe that her son was dead and remained a tireless – though heartbroken – campaigner. Maj was visited by the exiled Russian author, Alexander Solzhenitsyn, in 1974. He encouraged her to continue her efforts to free her son.

In *The Gulag Archipelago*, Solzhenitsyn had written of an encounter with a mysterious Swede with a fantastic story. Was this Raoul Wallenberg? One thing is clear: there was only one Swede still in a Soviet prison.

Maj pursued every possible lead until the time of her death in 1979. Simon Wiesenthal responded to her appeal to unveil further evidence. He stated, 'It is more important to find Raoul Wallenberg than to find any more Nazi war criminals.'

Mysterious encounters with a Swedish prisoner continued to trickle through, like a flickering face in the darkness around a campfire on the beach. Now you see him, now you don't. While some have been quick to dismiss these 'sightings', others have accepted their authenticity.

Professor Irwin Cotler was confident that Raoul was alive as recently as 1988, following a report he had heard during a meeting with Dr Andrei Sakharov.

Reports that Raoul had been living in a secret compound with others who have also been pronounced dead convinced the Czech nuclear physicist, Frantisek Jannouch, who declared that he thought it possible.

A confidential source told Kenne Fani, a former president of Sweden's largest film studio, that 'an old Scandinavian diplomat' who helped to save Jews in Budapest was treated for frostbite on his right foot at the hospital of a large Soviet prison camp in Blagoveshchensk, near the Chinese border, on 22 December 1986. Fani told the *New York Times* that he thought the man would have another name, but it could 'hardly be anyone else but Raoul Wallenberg'.

Following a six-month investigation, the *US News and World Report* published reports of new and credible witnesses who had seen Wallenberg after the date of his death. A cleaning woman named Varvara Larina, aged 72, was shown photographs of five men the same age as Raoul and asked to point out anyone she recalled. She had worked as a cleaning woman in Vladimir Prison, 120 miles northeast of Moscow, since 1945. 'She placed her finger firmly on the face of the Swede. She remembers him not by name but by cell number – 49 – where he was held in isolation.'

Three Polish witnesses who had been with Raoul much later than 1947 were also documented:

> After his repatriation to Poland, Boguslaw Baj read a newspaper report about Wallenberg's death and recognized the name and face. Baj died recently but his testimony is preserved in a documentary film.
>
> Baj's friend Josef Kowalski recalls first meeting Wallenberg at a Polish *Wigilya* – Christmas Eve service – held clandestinely at the camp. A Polish priest said a prayer, and the assembled sang carols. Kowalski says Wallenberg sat near him, but was taken off the transport before its final destination.

For over four decades the fate of Raoul Wallenberg remained a mystery, while all successive Russian leaders stuck to the official version of events. As for Raoul's driver, Vilmos Langfelder, the Kremlin informed the Hungarian government in 1957 that he too had died in Lubyanka Prison, in March 1948 ... of natural causes. Vilmos was known to be a healthy young man.

As Mikhail Gorbachev's era of *glasnost*, or openness, gathered momentum, it was evident that monumental changes were being experienced in the former Soviet Union. It was assumed that the clues in this mystery trail would lead us to the truth about Wallenberg, and hopefully to the man himself.

Per Anger was convinced that Raoul was alive in 1989. He listened in on a telephone conversation between Helmut Kohl and Mikhail Gorbachev as the German Chancellor pleaded with the Russian leader to 'let that old man go'.

Gorbachev was apparently unable to respond, but there were some significant developments. Russian media indicated that some actors in the drama were still alive and could be willing to talk, and in time several bit part players stepped from the shadows. A newspaper report linked the notorious Beria with Wallenberg's investigation, suggesting that he had handled the case personally.

The article claimed Beria suspected that Raoul was a party to German attempts to trade Hungarian Jews for urgently needed war materials from Britain, for use on the Eastern Front. This astonishing detail was denied in the West, but Soviet sources insist that at least one such deal was concluded through Switzerland, with the delivery of trucks to Hitler.

Perhaps the pinnacle of *glasnost* was reached in 1989 when Vadim Bakatin, the Minister of the Interior, invited Nina Lagergren and Guy von Dardel (Raoul's stepsister and brother) to Moscow for talks. After years of denial, the Russians produced Raoul's personal belongings. Suddenly, there it was: the proof of his presence inside Russia – his diplomatic passport, personal diary and address book, cigarette case, crumpled dollars and old Hungarian pengös, and a prison registration card stating that he had arrived there as a 'prisoner of war' on 6 February 1945.

The Russians told the family that the belongings had been found quite by chance some weeks earlier, in a box in the cellar at the Lubyanka Prison. Many Russian observers, including Professor Irwin Cotler, insist that it would have been impossible for the KGB to have stumbled across this collection in one location. Under established Soviet practice, such items would have been stored in four different places.

Raoul's family were also given the original handwritten report from Smoltsov regarding the death, and a television programme broadcast an appeal for information. Most who called were afraid to give their names and suggested meetings on street corners, but one man spoke openly. Alexander Smovsky, a 61-year-old biologist, had spent six years in various camps from 1949 to 1955. He said that he saw Raoul twice in a transit camp in Krasnoyark in Eastern Siberia and mentioned that Raoul was called 'the Baron', a nickname by which he had been known in Hungary.

The family were disappointed by the visit. Nina Lagergren told the press, 'They gave me the feeling that they [the Russians] must have much more. Everyone told us the Russians never destroy files and documents. They must be somewhere in the KGB.'

In October 1989, an international commission to investigate the Wallenberg case was set up and further discoveries were made. Log books at Lubyanka Prison had been inked out to conceal the names of Wallenberg and his driver, Vilmos Langfelder, as well as records of their interrogation. The logs had subsequently been restored and authenticated.

The logs revealed the name of Wallenberg's interrogator, identified as an NKVD Lieutenant-Colonel called Dimitri Kopylyansky, and showed that his last interrogation was on 11 March 1947, more than four months before his apparent death. While some have speculated that Kopylyansky played a part in Wallenberg's murder, when he was tracked down by the *Observer* newspaper the officer denied the charge. On the telephone he said, 'I never saw this man [Wallenberg] in my life.'

Meanwhile, Pavel Sudoplatov (described as a KGB hatchet man) published his autobiography with his own ideas about the mystery. Sudoplatov was close to both Stalin and Beria and revealed that the Soviet dictator wanted the Wallenbergs in Sweden to assist him in creating a neutral Finland. Marcus Wallenberg arranged a meeting in February 1944 between the Finnish Ambassador to Stockholm and a Soviet agent. By September, Finland had severed its alliance with Hitler and signed an armistice with the Soviet Union. Sudoplatov writes, 'Thus the detention of Raoul Wallenberg in Budapest was not accidental. Stalin and Molotov wanted to blackmail the Wallenberg family. They wanted to use its connections for favourable dealings with the West.'

Sudoplatov has his own hunch about Wallenberg's death. Outlining a scenario that could have been lifted from a spy thriller, he reveals the existence of a top-secret base known as Laboratory X, headed by Professor Grigori Moiseyevich Maironovsky. It was here, he asserted, that Wallenberg had been killed by lethal injection. While Sudoplatov's account seems possible, John Bierman has pointed out that the wily old KGB spy chief is not always the most credible reporter of events.

The Russians have not produced a death certificate or a report about a cremation. A prison registry recording deaths and suicides does not mention Wallenberg, although it lists a suicide attempt by a woman on the same date as his apparent death. Another official log has no mention of his name in the cremation list. The former head of Russia's central archive, Anatoly Prokopenko, has stated that official declarations proclaiming that they have no information are false. Per Anger continually registers the Soviet mania for producing numerous copies of documents for different departments.

While Russian leaders swap chairs, the search for the truth continues.

Boris Yeltsin announced the formation of a special commission to study the case. One of its members says he saw the file on

Mihail Tolstoy-Kutuzov, the Russian in Budapest suspected of being the Soviet agent who first identified Wallenberg. Aware that the file would reveal details of the arrest, the commission member was never allowed to read it. When Raoul's half-brother asked to see the file, he was told it no longer exists.

The KGB deny holding any further documentation on Wallenberg, but it is evident that they kept accurate records on most events. Russian journalist Alexandr Milchakov located 11 mass graves of Stalin's victims around Moscow. The KGB agreed to co-operate and open their archives, but they never did. However, a KGB officer assigned to help Milchakov said that, when he examined the documents for the period, he found that even the names of the victims dumped in the mass graves had been meticulously recorded.

Despite new openness, the suspicion is that considerable misinformation is still surfacing, as powerful officials try to cover up their roles in this shameful incident. Through the mist, just one fact emerges clearly: Raoul Wallenberg survived reports of his death in 1947.

Following Gorbachev's policy of openness, the former Soviet Union did release some information – but it took a little longer for *glasnost* to reach America.

In 1993, the CIA finally opened their files. Following a six-month investigation examining thousands of these freshly declassified documents, the *US News and World Report* concluded that Raoul Wallenberg had been an agent of American intelligence and that the Soviets jailed him, believing him to be an American spy working for the CIA. US officialdom abandoned him, making no attempt to secure his release, and Sweden never took up American offers of assistance. The newspaper's investigation concluded that the man who has been called 'the hero of the Holocaust' was betrayed.

The CIA report indicates that, alongside his mission for the War Refugee Board, Raoul was assigned to provide US intelligence with access to anti-Nazi resistance forces trying to break up Budapest's alliance with Berlin. For the OSS (forerunner to the CIA), Wallenberg was probably the only reliable man in wartime Budapest.

The CIA admitted that Wallenberg's link with the War Refugee Board and its 'clandestine character ... could have aroused Soviet suspicion and led to his disappearance'. Wallenberg's name appears on a roster of those who 'worked for the OSS in one capacity or another' and in a CIA memo from 1990, William Henhoeffer, curator of the CIA's Historical Intelligence Collection, stated that reports of Wallenberg's spy connections 'are essentially correct'. Iver Olsen, the man who hired Wallenberg, was stationed in Sweden for the OSS but had also undertaken some work for the War Refugee Board.

Tom Veres, Wallenberg's photographer, confirmed that he had driven the Swedish diplomat to Castle Hill to observe Russian gun positions. The Swedish diplomat was in touch with both the resistance and the Nazis and information was passed on to the US agents through Swedish diplomatic channels.

Governments that should have worked for his release had their own reasons to remain silent. The Swedes would not compromise their neutrality and admit that they had knowingly allowed one of their diplomats to work for the Americans. The Americans would not admit Soviet accusations that Wallenberg was working for them. If the US got involved, it would vindicate the Soviet charge that he had been a spy. This intrigue, compelling in its intensity, was Raoul Wallenberg's ironic reward from his political masters.

Laszlo Hertelendy worked with Wallenberg in Hungary to rescue Jews, but was muzzled by the Soviets, who 'surrounded me with a wall of silence'. In a *glasnost* interview with Budapest Radio, he provided a telltale clue about the Swede's activities in wartime Budapest. In this interview, Hertelendy declared that Wallenberg was a double agent. He worked for both the Americans and German intelligence. His original mission was to save specific Jews 'with family or business links to Sweden'. But Raoul decided early on to save as many as he could – by any means. He worked with German intelligence: 'in exchange for [American] information', he was allowed with Eichmann's knowledge to save the lives of Jews in 'a kind of quid pro quo'.

Susan Masinai agrees. In *Pack of Thieves*, by Richard Chesnoff, she suggests that Wallenberg was on assignment to several authorities and that each had a precise goal:

> Raoul had been charged with saving a specific 654 Jews, people who had been pre-eminent in pre-war Hungarian industry. I'm convinced that saving them may well have involved all sorts of under-the-table, strategic-material deals with the Germans. The Swedes, the Wallenberg family, and the US government felt these 654 people were needed to rebuild post-war Hungary. That Raoul saved so many others as well was his own doing, out of his own sense of sheer humanity.

Somewhere on the streets of Hungary, the job turned into a calling. Raoul Wallenberg had been tireless and reckless in his efforts to rescue those facing death. Nothing else mattered. It was as though he felt the burden of history and God propelling him forward.

The Russians undoubtedly knew about Wallenberg's links to the US intelligence network and were aware of his family connections. They probably knew of his assignment on behalf of the OSS and his links to Iver Olsen. With the Red Army drawing near to Hungary and German withdrawal gathering speed in the final hours of the war, orders had gone out to NKVD agents to bring him in.

Raoul Wallenberg was a marked man.

Chapter 18

THE SURVIVORS SPEAK

What happened to the survivors – the Jews of Budapest whom Wallenberg had rescued from the gates of hell?

Many had assumed that their saviour had died, but when the legend hit the international media in the late seventies, the response was remarkable. From all over the world, stories surfaced of Wallenberg's courage and heroism. Audiences were spellbound.

The *New York Times* reported an account of Simon Wisenthal's latest witness, Yury Belov, who had information on Wallenberg. Belov had been detained for 18 years in prisons, psychiatric hospitals and labour camps. At one time he was declared clinically dead. Alexander Solzhenitsyn reports that Belov was imprisoned 'to be cured of his belief in God'.

Belov reported that Wallenberg had been on hunger strike in 1961 in Moscow's Butyrki Prison and was transferred to a psychiatric hospital. Belov confirmed that the timing of this incident matched Professor Svartz's meeting with Professor Miashnikov.

The *New York Times* article stunned an American couple, Annette and Tom Lantos, both Hungarian Jews who had been saved by Wallenberg. When Tom was nominated as San Francisco's Representative to the US Congress, he introduced the bill that would make Raoul an honorary American citizen.

In Australia, the Wallenberg story also stirred one family. Ervin and Mary Forrester emigrated to Australia in 1950. They had decided to put the past behind them and never spoke of their history. 'It's difficult to relate war experiences to those who haven't lived through them,' Mrs Forrester explained. 'When I would start to talk about what we had gone through in Europe, an Australian neighbour would say how difficult it had been to cope with rationed butter.' Ervin Forrester was one of the estimated 600 Australians who had been saved by Wallenberg. When he learned in 1979 that Raoul had survived the war, he began talking more freely about his own past.[1]

Ervin Forrester was 19 years old in 1944 when he escaped being transported to a concentration camp. Recaptured, he was sentenced to death, but heard that the Swedish Embassy were giving passes to Jews. Mr Forrester claimed that he also had such a pass, but that it had been confiscated. To check his story, his captors telephoned the Swedish office and the call was transferred to Raoul Wallenberg. First, he took all the details from the Nazis about Forrester, to 'check his records'. Using this information, Wallenberg wrote out an official protective *Schutzpass* in the name of Ervin Forrester, and within an hour he was free.

In 1983, another survivor stepped from the shadows. For 37 years, Dr Vera Godkin, professor of French and English at Mercer County Community College, had kept her childhood a secret from everyone. As a child aged 12, she had been imprisoned, but escaped death through the intervention of one man: Raoul Wallenberg. When his story hit the headlines, Dr Godkin decided the time had come to honour his memory and to speak out. She said, 'Ever since 1983, when I began to speak of what happened, I realized that life will never be the same. The past has again come close enough to touch.'[2]

[1] Reported in the *Australian Jewish Times*, 9 May 1985.
[2] *Princeton Packet*, 1985.

In 1944, the 12-year-old Vera and her mother were imprisoned in Budapest when Wallenberg 'reminded' the prison commandant that the law did not permit the jailing of people under 14. The commandant was coerced into asking mothers if they wished their children to be released. Only Vera's mother let her child leave the prison.

Vera was then taken to a Swedish protected house in Budapest, to join other children who had been saved by Wallenberg. Three weeks later she contracted a severe case of scarlet fever and was transferred to the hospital for contagious diseases in the city. Vera continues the story: 'While I was there, the Hungarian SS broke into the home and kidnapped and killed all the children there.' In the meantime, Vera's mother was removed from prison and placed in a sealed cattle car on a train to Auschwitz. The train was halted on some pretext while the guards searched for an individual prisoner. During this delay, Vera's father slipped his wife a vial of poison, which she swallowed.

'She became unconscious and was carried off on a stretcher to a makeshift infirmary. Meanwhile, the Germans had discovered that the train was late. Deciding to make an example of this apparent malfunction, all the passengers were unloaded, crammed into a truck, and shot,' Vera explained.

Somehow, Vera's father escaped and made it to the Swedish Embassy in Budapest. There he met Raoul Wallenberg, who gave him a priceless *Schutzpass*. Vera continues, 'This pass put him under the protection of the Swedish Crown and allowed him and his family to live in one of Wallenberg's protected houses. Embassy officials knew I was in an orphanage, so my father finally found out his only child was alive. My mother, father and I were reunited and spent the last six weeks of the siege of Budapest in one of the protected houses.'

Veronica Laslo, a teenager in Budapest, now living in New York State, was also stirred by memories of the past. Veronica's family owned one of the biggest electric supply companies in the country, but her father was arrested and soon disappeared. Wallenberg came to the rescue. Veronica recalled, 'Wallenberg searched and my father was found – like an animal he was being walked [to the death camps].'

Veronica and her family had taken shelter in one of the Swedish protected houses when Arrow Cross gunmen broke in. 'My uncle and Wallenberg talked to the Nazis and gave them a month's food supply, and they left the Jews alone. Two weeks later, the German Nazis came in and insisted on lining us up and taking us, and that time Wallenberg gave the Nazis one [gold] coin for each person in the basement.'

In 1955 Tom Veres, Raoul's photographer in Budapest, escaped from Hungary. He arrived in America carrying one small suitcase and eventually made a career as a successful commercial photographer in New York State. 'When I escaped Hungary in 1955, I came here and told people about Wallenberg and they looked at me like I was crazy. They hadn't heard of him and they weren't interested … then one day I picked up the newspaper and there I saw my photographs.'

Veres told an American newspaper, 'Wallenberg was always "The Swede" with a capital "T". He was quiet, dignified, an all-business person in a wide-brimmed hat. He took the most extraordinary circumstances in a very calm manner.'

Veres once accompanied Wallenberg to a train station where Jews were being forced onto boxcars bound for the death camps. Wallenberg addressed the Nazi officers and called out for Jews carrying his special Swedish passport to leave the train. As hundreds poured out, Veres made his way to the back of the train, opened a door, and hundreds more jumped to the street and ran for their lives. Veres, however, was suddenly facing the barrel of a Nazi gun. Wallenberg called out to him to get into the car and they sped away. Veres says, 'I never jumped so big in my life.'

When the *Philadelphia Inquirer* published an article about Raoul in 1982, one reader was stirred into action. Louis Mermelstein had found that Wallenberg's *Schutzpass* was honoured by Nazi authorities in Czechoslovakia. Louis outlined his escape in a letter to the *Inquirer's* editor:

> My aunt, uncle and myself owe our lives to him. I jumped off a cattle car loaded with deportees to Auschwitz. Battered, bruised and without funds, I made my way to Zilana by the aid of two natives I met on the tracks. They issued me a *Schutzpass*, which satisfied the officials, giving me time to recover and to avoid re-arrest for the crime of being a Jew. I called the Jewish Council in Bratislava to inquire as to the whereabouts of my aunt and uncle who lived there. I found that they, too, were under Mr Wallenberg's protection.

In 1979, Yvonne Maria Singer sat spellbound in her kitchen in Toronto, Canada, as she read about an incident in Wallenberg's life as reported in her daily newspaper, the *Toronto Star*. Yvonne read that on a cold December night in Budapest in 1944, Tibor Vandor's young, pregnant wife went into labour. All hospitals were barred to Jews, but Raoul took the couple to his flat in Ostrom Street and invited them to make his bedroom their home. He tracked down a Jewish doctor to tend to Mrs Vandor, and then slept in a makeshift bed in the corridor of his apartment. He was awoken in the early hours of the morning to learn that a baby girl had been born. Raoul was named godfather to Yvonne Maria, a name chosen to honour one of his own grandmothers.

Yvonne read the story breathlessly, as she recognized the details of her own birth. Thirty-five years later the past had caught up with her. She was the child born in Wallenberg's bedroom. But Yvonne thought the story had been inaccurate on one critical point. Her parents were not Jews but Catholics. Greatly moved by the article, she telephoned the newspapers to correct this error.

The drama was far from over, however. To her incredulity, she learned that her parents had never told their daughter of their true heritage, determining that it was in her best interests to be raised a Christian. Ironically, in her youth, she had met and fallen in love with a young Jewish boy, but had been forbidden to marry him. In defiance, she had proceeded with the marriage and converted to Judaism, long before she learned the truth about her childhood.

Sister Marie Catherine, the mother superior of a convent in Rimont, southeast France, was to have a similarly poignant experience the same year. After a visit to Bethlehem and the Wailing Wall in Jerusalem, she returned to France deeply moved. She described her feelings to her mother, Mrs Emma Szentes, who then lived in Switzerland. Mrs Szentes had been a secretary to Raoul in Budapest, and both mother and daughter had been protected by his *Schutzpass* and had lived in one of his safe houses.

As Sister Marie shared these deep feelings with her mother, a secret was unveiled. Mrs Szentes told her daughter, 'I'm going to tell you something that I've never told anybody for more than 40 years, even my children ... Although we are a Hungarian Catholic family, we are of Jewish origin. In 1938, when we understood the danger of Nazism, we converted to Christianity.'

After being raised from childhood as a Catholic, Sister Marie was overwhelmed by this discovery. Today, she has changed her name to Miriam and obtained permission for her order to be known as 'The Little Sisters of Israel'. Miriam explained, 'The apostles lived in exactly the same way in the early years of the Church. They went to the synagogues while teaching the gospel.'

Tommy Lapid was rescued when he was 13 years old and was one of 900 people crowded 15 or 20 to a room in one of Raoul's protected houses. He later became director-general of the Israeli Broadcasting Authority in Jerusalem. He shared his recollections with John Bierman:

We were hungry, thirsty, and frightened all the time and we were more afraid of the Arrow Cross than of the British, American, and Russian bombardments put together. Those people had guns and they thought the least they could do for the war effort was to kill a few Jews before the Russians got there, so they were entering these houses, which were undefended, and carrying people away. We were very close to the Danube and we heard them shooting people into the river all night.

I sometimes think that the greatest achievement of the Nazis was that we just accepted the fact that we were destined to be killed. My father was in Mauthausen concentration camp and perished there. I, an only child, stayed with my mother. I kept asking her for bread. I was so hungry. (Years later, if there was no bread in the house, she would get out of bed at night and go down to a café and ask for two slices of bread – although then a very well-to-do lady in Tel Aviv, she had to have some bread in the house because of those days when she couldn't supply me with any.)

One morning, a group of these Hungarian fascists came into the house and said all the able-bodied women must go with them. We knew what this meant. My mother kissed me and I cried and she cried. We knew we were parting forever and she left me there, an orphan, to all intents and purposes. Then, two or three hours later, to my amazement, my mother returned with the other women. It seemed like a mirage, a miracle. My mother was there – she was alive and she was hugging me and kissing me, and she said one word: 'Wallenberg.'

I knew who she meant because Wallenberg was a legend among the Jews. In the complete and total hell in which we lived, there was a saviour-angel somewhere, moving around. After she had composed herself, my mother told me that they were being taken to the river when a car arrived and out stepped Wallenberg – and they knew immediately who it was, because there was only one such person in the world. He went up to the Arrow Cross leader and protested that the women were under his protection. They argued with him, but he must have had incredible charisma, some great personal authority, because there was absolutely nothing behind him, nothing to back him up. He stood out there in the street, probably feeling the loneliest man in the world, trying to pretend there was something behind him. They could have shot him there and then in the street and nobody would have known about it. Instead, they relented and let the women go.[3]

Miriam Herzog was a teenager when she was forced to join the death march. She recalled for John Bierman those awesome moments when her life hung by a thread:

The conditions were frightful. We walked thirty to forty kilometres a day in freezing rain, driven on all the time by the Hungarian gendarmes. We were all women and girls. I was 17 at the time. The gendarmes were brutal, beating those who could not keep up, leaving others to die in the ditches. It was terrible for the older women. Sometimes at night we didn't have any shelter, let alone anything to eat or drink. One night we stopped in a square in the middle of a village. We just lay down on the ground to rest. There was a frost in the night and in the morning many of the older women were dead. It was so cold, it was as though we were frozen into the ground. The thirst was even worse than the hunger.

I didn't have a Swedish passport, but I thought it was worth a try and I had this tremendous will to survive, even though I was so weak from dysentery and wretched from the dirt and the lice that infested me, that all I could do was find a space on the floor and lie down. I don't know how much later it was — maybe days — but suddenly I heard a great commotion among the women. 'It's Wallenberg,' they said. I didn't know this name, but somebody told me he was a Swedish diplomat who had saved many Jews already. I didn't think he could really help me, and anyway I was

[3] John Bierman, *Righteous Gentile* (Allen Lane, 1981).

now too weak to move, so I lay there on the floor as dozens of women clustered around him. He said to them: 'Please, you must forgive me, but I cannot help all of you. I can only provide certificates for a hundred of you.' Then he said something which really surprised me. He said: 'I feel I have a mission to save the Jewish nation and so I must rescue the young ones first.' I had never heard of the idea of a Jewish nation before. Jewish people, of course, but not a Jewish nation. Later I was to think about this quite a lot. Anyway, he looked around the room and began putting names down on a list, and when he saw me lying on the floor he came over to me. He asked my name and added it to the list. After a day or two, the hundred of us whose names had been taken were moved out and put into a cattle truck on a train bound for Budapest. We were warned to keep quiet *en route*, because if we were discovered we might all be sent back to Auschwitz. I don't know how Wallenberg managed it; I suppose he must have bribed the railway officials and guards. Because the railway lines had been bombed, the journey back to Budapest took three days, instead of three or four hours, and we were in a terrible state when we arrived. There were a lot more dangers and hardships ahead of us, but we were alive — and it was thanks entirely to Wallenberg.[4]

[4] Ibid.

Conclusion

Raoul Wallenberg was the lonely voice of justice in a world aflame. He fought evil because it was there. There was no other choice. He risked his life because the Jews, 'his people', God's people, had to be saved.

He was an inspiration to those around him, as he must be to the generations that follow.

Today, we witness countless atrocities. We see, in living colour, in our homes, brutal examples of collective homicide, man's inhumanity to man, the degradation and devastation of men, women and children, in war zones and desolate lands. We sometimes feel alone, powerless. What can one person do?

Raoul Wallenberg was just one person. Alone, against all odds, he confronted the technicians of genocide. Alone, against all odds, he saved thousands of Jews from the fires of Auschwitz.

While Steven Spielberg's *Schindler's List* reminded us that many courageous individuals saved Jewish lives, the story of Raoul Wallenberg has no equal in the history of the Holocaust. Larger than life, he seemed invincible, indefatigable.

Does the story yet have an ending? All the evidence indicates that Raoul Wallenberg was still alive after 1947, the date of his apparent death. Adrift on the archipelago of the Gulag system. In a cell in the heart of a Russian prison. Secluded in solitary silence. Waiting.

He had every reason to expect both the Swedish and the American governments to exert greater pressure to secure his release. His sense of betrayal, when he realized that there would be no escape from his living torment, must have been devastating.

Will we ever know the truth about Raoul Wallenberg? Perhaps that depends on how seriously we ask the question.

The KGB probably hid the Wallenberg case from the Kremlin, not an unlikely scenario by any intelligence agency. The missing Wallenberg file may have been destroyed in the cover-up. Tracing Wallenberg is made difficult when it is probable that, like many foreign prisoners, he has been given another name or could be referred to only by a number. The task ahead is formidable.

Documents and reports released following *glasnost* provide a few nuggets of truth. Hopefully, in time, the movement of the earth will loosen an unlikely stone.

While his fate remains unknown, careful consideration should be given to any memorial or epitaph. Although each passing day reduces the chance of him entering our midst, every possible effort must be made to rescue him and to honour his life's work before we finally close the gate.

The international Christian community must remember him and pay tribute to him. The children of God must hold him in their hearts and emulate this man who fought tirelessly and self-lessly for justice. We must ensure that his memory will never fade and that his name symbolizes that epic struggle against tyranny and evil.

It is up to all of us to fight for Wallenberg's liberty, either until such time as he is able to walk freely amongst us once again, or until his memory can finally be laid to rest with all the honours and love that it deserves.

We owe it to him.

We owe it to ourselves.

We owe it to our children and their generation.

Last Report from
Raoul Wallenberg in Budapest
8 December 1944

Since my last report the situation of the Hungarian Jews has noticeably deteriorated. About 40,000 Jews, comprising 15,000 members of the Jewish Forced Labour Corps and 25,000 other persons of both sexes were apprehended in their homes or in the streets and forced to set out for Germany on foot. The distance to be covered was approximately 240 kilometres. Since these marches were arranged, the weather has turned cold and rainy. People sleep in the open without the slightest shelter. Most of them were given food and drink no more than three or four times. Many of them died. The undersigned was able to establish the fact that in Moson-Magyarovar seven persons died one day and seven the previous day. The Secretary of the Portuguese Legation saw 42 corpses in one road and Deputy Prime Minister Szöllössy admitted that he saw two corpses. Those not able to march any further were shot on the spot. At the frontier they were received by SS Commander Eichmann, thrashed and ill-treated and led to work in the trenches and fortifications. The enclosed photos 1 and 2 show civilians ready to continue the march, 3 shows members of the Jewish Forced Labour Corps and 4 shows two girls before and after their march from Budapest to Hegyeshalom.

20,000 members of the Jewish Forced Labour Corps were taken to the frontier by train. As a rule they worked on

Hungarian territory. A photo showing the work of the Swedish Rescue Commission is enclosed. The entrenchment work mentioned in the last report has since ceased.

The Jews have been crammed into a central ghetto supposed to accommodate 69,000 persons — but in actual fact probably containing many more — further into an international ghetto for 17,000 persons, which already harbours 33,000. Of these 7,000 are in Swedish, 2,000 in Red Cross and 23,000 in Swiss houses. Several thousand Jews under Swiss and Vatican protection were dragged away to be deported or were transferred to the Central ghetto. In the ghetto, four to 12 Jews share a room, in the Swedish houses the situation is still the most favourable.

A dysentery epidemic of not too serious a nature has broken out among the Jews. In the Swiss houses, the state of health of the Jews is still good, only five persons having died up to now. This department inoculates all protected Jews against typhoid, paratyphoid and cholera. The staff too will be inoculated in due course.

As a rule, Jewish property has been badly looted, as the Jews were only allowed to take as much with them as they could carry. The food situation will shortly be catastrophic.

A great number of Jews were kidnapped by the Arrow Cross, who ill-treat and torture them on their premises before passing them on for deportation.

Rumours are circulating, according to which the Death Brigade, closely associated with Minister Kovarcs, is preparing to incite a pogrom. I do not believe that this pogrom will spread very far, as for instance the SS organs have received no orders to arrange a systematic mass-murder of the Jews.

Organization: After the heavy blow of October, this department has been greatly strengthened. There are 335 employees as well as 40 doctors, house-wardens etc. All these, together with their families amounting to about the same number, live on the premises of the department. In all, 10 houses are used for offices and living accommodation, one of which is in the International ghetto.

Two hospitals were set up, respectively improvised, providing altogether 150 beds. A soup kitchen was installed as well. The Jews of the Swedish-protected houses hand their ration-cards to the department, which collects the provisions and distributes them.

A great part of the department's correspondence was destroyed. The provision department has bought food to the value of about 2 million pengös.

Results achieved: The department succeeded in obtaining passes from the Honved Ministry with the aid of which all Jews employed in forced labour but in possession of foreign documents can be sent back to Budapest.

A delegate of the department set out by car and distributed these passes. Soon after, some 15,000 Jews returned to Budapest.

The columns *en route* for the frontier were sporadically supplied with food and medicines. About 200 sick persons were collected from the deportation assembly centres by ambulance and brought back to Budapest.

It was possible to rescue some 2,000 persons from deportation through intervening for some reason or the other. Of these, 500 were actually rescued from Hegyeshalom. Unfortunately this had to stop, as the German members of the Eichmann Commando threatened to use violence and force.

Up to now Jews in possession of Swedish safe-conducts have been treated leniently in comparison with those enjoying the protection of other neutral powers. As far as can be ascertained, only 10 Jews with Swedish safe-conducts have up to now been shot in and around Budapest.

Budapest, December 8th, 1944
(sgd.) Raoul Wallenberg
Secretary of Legation

Appendix 2

OFFICIAL SOVIET STATEMENTS ABOUT THE DISAPPEARANCE OF RAOUL WALLENBERG
1945–57

16 January 1945

Wallenberg is in Soviet hands.

Soviet Deputy Foreign Minister, Vladimir Dekanosov

February 1945

Wallenberg is in the USSR.

Soviet Ambassador to Sweden, Alexandra Kollontai

8 March 1945

Wallenberg was murdered by Hungarian fascists or by agents of the Gestapo. *Soviet-controlled Kossuth Radio in Budapest*

18 August 1947

Wallenberg is not in the Soviet Union and is unknown to us.

Soviet Deputy Foreign Minister, Andrei Vishinsky

5 August 1953

Wallenberg has not been and is not in the Soviet Union and is unknown to us. *Soviet Ambassador, Konstantin Rodionov*

18 March 1956

A thorough investigation has confirmed that Wallenberg was not and has never been in the USSR. *Soviet Foreign Ministry*

5 April 1956

We will study the documents handed to us by Prime Minister Erlander of Sweden. If it arises that Wallenberg was in the Soviet Union, he would naturally be allowed to come home.

Soviet communiqué after a meeting between Erlander and Krushchev

2 February 1957

In pursuance of the Swedish Government's request, the Soviet Government instructed the pertinent Soviet authorities to pursue the material concerning Raoul Wallenberg which had been received from the Swedish quarters at the Swedish-Soviet negotiations in Moscow ... In the course of perusal and testing of said material, the Soviet authorities have made a careful search of the archives ... similarly many persons have been questioned who could have had nothing to do with circumstances mentioned in the material received from Sweden.

As a result, it has not been possible to find any information whatsoever concerning Wallenberg's sojourn in the Soviet Union. It has transpired that none of those heard knew of any person by the name of Wallenberg. In this connection, the competent Soviet authorities have undertaken to search page by page the archive documents from all wards in certain prisons. As a result of such search of archive documents from the health service in the Lubyanka Prison, a document has been found which there is good reason to consider as referring to Raoul Wallenberg.

This document has the form of a handwritten report, addressed to the former minister of state security of the Soviet Union, Abakumov, and written in the hand of the health service director of said prison, A. I. Smoltsov, reading as follows:

'I report that the prisoner Walenberg [sic], who is well known to you, died suddenly in his cell last night, probably as the result of a heart attack. Persuant to instructions given by you that I have Walenberg under my care, I request approval to make an autopsy with a view to establishing a cause of death. Smoltsov, Chief of Prison Sanitary Ward, July 17, 1947, Colonel in Medicine Service.'

On this report the following notation is found in Smoltsov's handwriting:

'I have personally notified the Minister and it has been ordered that the body be cremated without an autopsy. (signed) Smoltsov.'

It has not been possible to find any other information whatsoever having the character of document of testimony, all the more so since the aforementioned A. I. Smoltsov died on May 7, 1953. On the strength of what has been cited above, the conclusion should be drawn that Wallenberg died in July 1947.

Wallenberg was apparently arrested along with other persons in the area for military operations by Soviet troops. At the same time it may be considered indisputable that Wallenberg's subsequent detention in prison, as well as the incorrect information about him supplied by certain leaders of the security organs of the Soviet Union's Foreign Ministry over a period of years, comprised the result of Abakumov's criminal activities. In connection with gross crimes committed by him it will be recalled that Abakumov, who engaged in activities implying the violations of the laws of the Soviet Union, and who had sought to inflict upon the Soviet Union all kinds of damage, was executed in accordance with the verdict handed down by the Supreme Court of the Soviet Union.

The Soviet Government presents its sincere regrets because of what has occurred and expresses its profound sympathy to the Swedish Government as well as to Raoul Wallenberg's relatives.

Andrei Gromyko
Deputy Foreign Minister

Bibliography

Several publications and books were of particular help, including the following:

John Bierman, *Righteous Gentile* (Allen Lane, 1981)

Richard Breitman, *Official Secrets* (Allen Lane, 1998)

Richard Z. Chesnoff, *Pack of Thieves* (Weidenfeld & Nicolson, 1999)

Lucy Dawidowicz, *The War Against the Jews 1933–1945* (Penguin Books, 1975)

Martin Gilbert, *Auschwitz and the Allies* (Michael Joseph and George Rainbird, 1981)

Leonard Gross, *The Last Jews in Berlin* (Simon & Schuster, 1982)

Rudolf Hoess, *Commandant of Auschwitz* (Weidenfeld & Nicolson, 1959)

The Holocaust (Yad Vashem studies, Volume 5, 1963)

Walter Laqueur, *The Terrible Secret* (Penguin Books, 1980)

Elenore Lester, *The Man in the Iron Web* (Prentice-Hall, 1982)

Dr Miklos Nyiszli, *Auschwitz* (Panther Books, 1962)

Kati Marton, *Wallenberg* (Random House, 1982)

William L. Shirer, *The Rise and Fall of the Third Reich* (Secker & Warburg, 1960)

J.P. Stern, *Hitler* (Fontana, 1975)

Swedish Foreign Office White Books on Raoul Wallenberg
(Swedish Foreign Ministry, Stockholm, 1980)
Raoul Wallenberg, *Letters and Dispatches 1924–1944*
(Arcade Publishing, 1995)
Frederick E. Werbell and Thurston Clarke, *Lost Hero*
(McGraw-Hill, 1982)

Danny Smith is the director of Jubilee Action, a human rights charity. For David Amess MP's speech about Raoul Wallenberg in Parliament and other selected documents, please write to:

Jubilee Action
St Johns
Cranleigh Road
Wonersh
Guildford
Surrey
GU5 0QX

Telephone: +44 1483 894787
Fax: +44 1483 894797
Email: info@jubileeaction.co.uk

Christian Books

Timeless truths in shifting times

www.christian-publishing.com

News from a Christian perspective

Exclusive author interviews

Read extracts from the latest books

Share thoughts and faith

Complete list of signing events

Full catalogue & ordering

www.christian-publishing.com

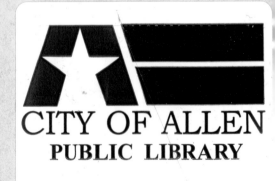